Bible
Speaks
today

the message of

MALACHI

Series editors:
Alec Motyer (OT)
John Stott (NT)
Derek Tidball (Bible Themes)

the message of

MALACHI

'I have loved you,' says the Lord
Revised edition

Peter Adam

Academic
An imprint of InterVarsity Press
Downers Grove, Illinois

InterVarsity Press USA
P.O. Box 1400 | Downers Grove, IL 60515-1426, USA
ivpress.com | email@ivpress.com

Inter-Varsity Press, England
Studio 101, The Record Hall, 16–16A Baldwins Gardens | London, EC1N 7RJ, UK
ivpbooks.com | ivp@ivpbooks.com

InterVarsity Press® is the publishing division of InterVarsity Christian Fellowship/USA®. For more information, visit intervarsity.org.

Inter-Varsity Press, England, originated within the Inter-Varsity Fellowship, now the Universities and Colleges Christian Fellowship, a student movement connecting Christian Unions in universities and colleges throughout Great Britain, and a member movement of the International Fellowship of Evangelical Students.

Unless otherwise stated, Scripture quotations are from the Holy Bible, New International Version (Anglicised edition). Copyright © 1979, 1984, 2011 by Biblica. Used by permission of Hodder & Stoughton, an Hachette company. All rights reserved. 'NIV' is a registered trademark of Biblica, UK trademark number 1448790.

This edition published 2024.

Cover design: Cindy Kiple
Images: © MarkSkalny / iStock / Getty Images Plus

USA ISBN 978-1-5140-0657-3 (print) | USA ISBN 978-1-5140-0658-0 (digital)
UK ISBN 978-1-78974-449-1 (print) | UK ISBN 978-1-78359-629-4 (digital)

Typeset in Great Britain by CRB Associates, Potterhanworth, Lincolnshire

Printed in the United States of America ∞

Library of Congress Cataloging-in-Publication Data
A catalog record for this book is available from the Library of Congress.

British Library Cataloguing-in-Publication Data
A catalogue record for this book is available from the British Library.

30 29 28 27 26 25 24 | 8 7 6 5 4 3 2 1

Dedicated, with deep gratitude, to those who have wrestled in prayer for me and for my ministry, and for those who continue to do so

Contents

Bible Speaks Today

GENERAL PREFACE

The Bible Speaks Today describes three series of expositions, based on the books of the Old and New Testaments, and on Bible themes that run through the whole of Scripture. Each series is characterized by a threefold ideal:

- to expound the biblical text with accuracy
- to relate it to contemporary life, and
- to be readable.

These books are, therefore, not 'commentaries', for the commentary seeks rather to elucidate the text than to apply it, and tends to be a work rather of reference than of literature. Nor, on the other hand, do they contain the kinds of 'sermons' that attempt to be contemporary and readable without taking Scripture seriously enough. The contributors to The Bible Speaks Today series are all united in their convictions that God still speaks through what he has spoken, and that nothing is more necessary for the life, health and growth of Christians than that they should hear what the Spirit is saying to them through his ancient – yet ever modern – Word.

ALEC MOTYER
JOHN STOTT
DEREK TIDBALL
Series editors

Author's preface

I have loved the book of Malachi for many years, and have taught and preached it many times. I am grateful for those who have patiently listened to my teaching, and prompted my thinking further with their perceptive questions. I am especially grateful to the people of St Jude's Carlton, who heard series of sermons in 1983 and 1998, to the preaching conference at the Sydney Missionary and Bible College in 1997, members of the Queensland branch of the Church Missionary Society in 2001, students at Ridley Melbourne in 2005, and participants at the Evangelical Ministry Assembly in 2006.

I am also grateful to Philip Duce and Alec Motyer for their invitation to write this book, and to include it in The Bible Speaks Today series. I have always valued this series, so it is good to be part of it.

My thanks for practical help to Ruth Millard, librarian of the Leon Morris Library at Ridley Melbourne, and to Annabelle Crane and Peter Williams.

As I have been writing this book, I have realized how much I have learnt from others in every area of life, and how enriched I have been by these acts of generosity. This has encouraged me to see the value of teaching others, and has made me very grateful to God, the giver of every good and perfect gift.

PETER ADAM

Select bibliography

Where these books are cited in the notes, it is by author and title only.

Baldwin, J. G., *Haggai, Zechariah, Malachi,* Tyndale Old Testament Commentaries (London: Tyndale Press, 1972).

Barnett, P., *The Second Epistle to the Corinthians,* New International Commentary on the New Testament (Grand Rapids: Eerdmans, 1997).

Benton, J., *Losing Touch with the Living God* (Welwyn/Darlington: Evangelical Press, 1985).

Calvin, J., *Commentary on Isaiah 1 – 32,* Calvin's Commentaries, vol. 7 (Grand Rapids: Baker, 1981 [1843]).

——, *Habakkuk, Zephaniah, Haggai, Zechariah, Malachi,* Calvin's Commentaries, vol. 15 (Grand Rapids: Baker, 1981 [1848]).

——, *The Institutes of the Christian Religion,* vols. 1 and 2, tr. Ford Lewis Battles, in *The Library of Christian Classics,* vols. 20 and 21 (Philadelphia: The Westminster Press, 1960).

Carson, D. A., 'Matthew', in F. E. Gaebelein (ed.), *The Expositor's Bible Commentary,* vol. 8 (Grand Rapids: Regency, 1984).

Craigie, P. C., *Twelve Prophets,* Daily Bible Study Series, vol. 2 (Edinburgh: Saint Andrew Press; Philadelphia: Westminster, 1985).

Glazier-McDonald, B., *Malachi: The Divine Messenger,* SBL Dissertation 98 (Atlanta: Scholars Press, 1987).

Hill, A. E., *Malachi,* Anchor Commentaries 25D (New York: Doubleday, 1998).

Jacobs, M. R., 'Malachi', in K. J. Vanhoozer (ed.), *Theological Interpretation of the Old Testament* (Grand Rapids: Baker Academic; London: SPCK, 2008), pp. 305–312.

Kaiser, W. C., *Malachi: God's Unchanging Love* (Grand Rapids: Baker, 1984).

Mason, R., *The Books of Haggai, Zechariah and Malachi*, Cambridge Bible Commentary (Cambridge: Cambridge University Press, 1977).

Moore, T. V., *Haggai and Malachi*, Geneva Series Commentary (Edinburgh: Banner of Truth, 1960 [1856]).

Pohlig, J. N., *An Exegetical Summary of Malachi* (Dallas: SIL, 1998).

Smith, R. L., *Micah–Malachi*, Word Biblical Commentary 32 (Waco: Word, 1984).

Verhoef, P. A., *The Books of Haggai and Malachi*, New International Commentary on the Old Testament (Grand Rapids: Eerdmans, 1987).

Wenham, G. J., *The Book of Leviticus*, New International Commentary on the Old Testament (Grand Rapids: Eerdmans, 1979).

Introduction

1. Malachi: book and prophet

The book of Malachi sits aptly in our Bibles as the last book of the Old Testament, for it looks back to the Old Testament and assumes, summarizes and applies its message. But it also looks forward to the New Testament, with its promises of the coming reign of God.

One of the book's most striking features is the way in which every word of God is contradicted or questioned by God's people. This is the deep structure of the book, and its recurring theme. Contradicting God and his words was unfortunately characteristic of this contrary people! Whatever God said, they contradicted by questions. Here are examples:

'I have loved you,' says the LORD.
'But you ask, "How have you loved us?"'
(1:2–3)

It is you priests who show contempt for my name.
But you ask, 'How have we shown contempt for your name?'
By offering defiled food on my altar.
But you ask, 'How have we defiled you?'
(1:6–7)

You have wearied the LORD with your words.
'How have we wearied him?' you ask.
By saying, 'All who do evil are good in the eyes of the LORD, and he is pleased with them' or 'Where is the God of justice?'
(2:17)

'Return to me, and I will return to you,' says the LORD Almighty.
'But you ask, "How are we to return?"
'Will a mere mortal rob God? Yet you rob me.
'But you ask, "How are we robbing you?"'
(3:7–8)

'You have spoken arrogantly against me,' says the LORD.
'Yet you ask, "What have we said against you?"'
(3:13)

We see here the persistence of God in speaking to his people, and also the gap between what God thinks and what the people think. God through the prophet reveals his thoughts, and contrasts them by articulating the thoughts and words of his people. In this book we have a clear picture of grace and sin in close proximity.

Another striking feature is that God's people appear to be serving God reluctantly, in a half-hearted kind of way. They are neither energetic enough to serve him wholeheartedly, nor to engage in blatant disobedience. It is hardly satisfactory for them, as it is hardly satisfactory for God!

We may find ourselves in a church like that, in which case Malachi is a very apt book. But even in the case of a church full of young enthusiastic believers, who need restraining not goading, Malachi is still useful as a warning for the future, or as training in ministry to people who are more half-hearted.

The word Malachi means 'my messenger', which is a good name for a prophet. Some think that it is not a name but a title, but I assume here that it is the prophet's name.

Malachi prophesied after the people of God had returned from exile in Babylon and settled in Jerusalem and Judah. The temple has been rebuilt (1:10), and there is a (Persian) governor (1:8). Though no date is given for the prophecy, the problem of divorce (2:10–16) was also present in the time of Ezra and Nehemiah (Ezra 9 – 10; Neh. 13:23–27). And reluctance to provide for the temple in Malachi (1:6–14) is also present in Nehemiah 13:10–13. So it looks as if Malachi prophesied around that time, though his name is not mentioned in Ezra or Nehemiah, although these books do mention Haggai and Zechariah (see Ezra 6:14). (See the table opposite.)

Malachi probably gave his prophecy sometime between 460 and 400 BC.

Date BC	Kings of Babylon, then Persia	God's people	Bible books
597–587	Nebuchadnezzar	Jerusalem and the temple destroyed, the people taken to exile in Babylon	Jeremiah and Ezekiel
587–539	Nebuchadnezzar and Belshazzar	In exile in Babylon	Daniel
539	Cyrus, king of Persia, conquered Babylon	The first group returned to Jerusalem from Babylon, and the temple was rebuilt	Haggai and Zechariah
530	Cambyses conquered Egypt		
522	Darius I		
485	Xerxes/Ahasuerus		Esther
465	Artaxerxes	458 The second group returned, led by Ezra	Malachi?
445		The third group returned, led by Nehemiah. The walls of Jerusalem were rebuilt	Malachi?
433		Nehemiah returned to Jerusalem after a short visit to Babylon	
After 433			Ezra and Nehemiah? Malachi?

2. Malachi for us today

There are three ways in which this book is the word of the Lord for us today.

First, Malachi saw that at the heart of God's people, the church, must lie a deep, radical and overwhelming conviction that God loves them. Without this at our heart, we are lost.

Second, Malachi knew that the greatest sin of God's people is the sin against God. We easily get confused about sin. We see that we can sin against ourselves, and harm ourselves. We see that we can sin against others, and harm them. But we find it harder to take seriously our sin against God. Yet here is the fundamental sin, the source of all sin.

Third, in Malachi's day the people of God were in a mess. While they were not actually running away from God, and were not worshipping idols, as they had in the past, they seemed to lack the energy to serve God wholeheartedly. They tried to live in neutral territory, neither serving God too enthusiastically, nor turning away from God too enthusiastically. In this they were self-deceived. They thought they were in a grey no-man's land, where they neither needed to respond wholeheartedly to God, nor refuse him. In fact they were in a vicious circle, a terrifying whirlpool, sinking further and further to destruction. Malachi is God's effective remedy for such a situation among the people of God.

3. Features of this exposition

Following the general pattern of volumes in The Bible Speaks Today series, I have had three priorities in mind.

a. The Old Testament as a prophecy of Christ

When the apostle Paul wrote to Timothy, he explained in a simple phrase the message of the Old Testament, which Timothy had known from an early age, taught no doubt by his grandmother Lois and mother Eunice. He wrote, 'From infancy you have known the Holy Scriptures, which are able to make you wise for salvation through faith in Christ Jesus' (2 Tim. 3:15). The Old Testament is about salvation through faith in Jesus Christ. It is more than this, but it is not less than this.

The Old Testament pointed forward to Christ in many ways: these include prophecies, both general and specific; a people who do Christ-like actions and fulfil Christ-like roles, such as prophets, priests and kings; rituals such as sacrifices; and places and buildings such as the land, tabernacle and temple. These all served God's purpose in their day, and also promised and pointed forward to Christ: Christ fulfilled their promise, and was the substantial fulfilment which they foreshadowed. It is biblical theology which unpacks these themes in the Bible. The two challenges for expositors today are not to reduce the Old Testament to this prophetic function, and not to miss this part of its purpose.

We see this prophetic use very clearly in the teaching of the Lord Jesus. He explained his identity and mission through his interpretation of the Old Testament, and expected his disciples to see him in the words of the Old Testament.

> He said to them, 'How foolish you are, and how slow to believe all that the prophets have spoken! Did not the Messiah have to suffer these things and then enter his glory?' And beginning with Moses and all the Prophets, he explained to them what was said in all the Scriptures concerning himself.
> (Luke 24:25–27)

b. The Old Testament as training in godliness and ministry

A similar use of the Old Testament was to train Christian leaders and equip them for ministry, according to Paul: 'All Scripture is God-breathed and is useful for teaching, rebuking, correcting and training in righteousness, so that the servant of God may be thoroughly equipped for every good work' (2 Tim. 3:16–17). And when Paul wrote to the Corinthians he warned them from the history of God's people in their wilderness wanderings after the exodus:

> Now these things occurred as examples to keep us from setting our hearts on evil things as they did . . . These things happened to them as examples and were written down as warnings for us, on whom the culmination of the ages has come.
> (1 Cor. 10:6, 11)

These happened to them, but were written down for us. Of course these things were written down for subsequent generations of Old Testament believers, but they were written down for us as well. Similarly, the author of Hebrews quoted the Old Testament as part of his own exhortation to Christian believers:

> And have you completely forgotten this word of encouragement that addresses you as a father addresses his son? It says,
> 'My son, do not make light of the Lord's discipline,
> and do not lose heart when he rebukes you,
> because the Lord disciplines the one he loves,
> and he chastens everyone he accepts as his son.'
> (Heb. 12:5–6, quoting Prov. 3:11–12)

We can see that these two great purposes, the prophetic and the moral, are not mutually contradictory. In 2 Timothy 3, as we have seen, Paul identifies one purpose of Scripture as being to make us wise for salvation through faith in Jesus Christ, and in the next two verses he also explains the moral and educational value of Scripture (2 Tim. 3:15–17). What God has joined together we should not separate!

c. Malachi addressed the people of God

It is also significant that Malachi, like most books in the Bible, was addressed to the people of God, the church of that day, and not to individuals.

Those of us who live in the Western world have been brainwashed into individualism. We think and feel as individuals, we regard individuals as the most important form of human life, we privilege individuals over communities, and so we read and preach the Bible as if it was addressed to individuals.

There are some books that are addressed to individuals, for example Luke and Acts, and Paul's letters to Timothy, Titus and Philemon. However, most books of the Bible address the people of God, whether in the Old Testament or the New. So Deuteronomy is a collection of sermons to Israel as a nation, and all the Old Testament prophets addressed the people of God as a whole, even if some specific prophecies were given to individuals. Paul wrote most of his letters to churches. Paul's letters to Timothy and Titus are primarily about the life of the churches, and his letter to Philemon was also addressed 'to the church that meets in your home' (Philm. 2). And of course, although Luke wrote Luke and Acts for Theophilus (Luke 1:1–4; Acts 1:1), it was a practice of the day to dedicate writings to an important person with a wider audience in mind.

This means that if we read or preach Malachi and apply it to us as individuals only, we will miss an important element of the message. 'Scripture is God preaching',[1] and part of this sermon is the book Malachi. We should follow what God has done, and address this book to the church of our day. Our first question should be, 'What is God saying to us?', not, 'What is God saying to me?' or 'What is God saying to individuals in the congregation?'

So, rather than looking for individual application, we should work for corporate application. 'Corporate' here does not mean big business, it means 'body', as in 'the body of Christ'. We should train ourselves to look for the shared values of our churches, our shared godliness, our shared sins, our shared blind spots, our shared weaknesses, our shared strengths.

Let's take as examples two issues from Malachi: robbing God, and speaking harsh words against God (3:8–15). The first is more than 'How do we as individuals rob God?', but 'How are we as a church robbing God?', 'How is our church letting individuals rob God and not challenging them?', 'How is my robbing God setting a bad example to others in the church?', 'What am I doing to challenge the church as a whole to stop robbing God?' and 'What are our church leaders doing to stop individuals and the church as a whole robbing God?'

Similarly, the second issue is more than 'How do we as individuals speak harsh words against God?' We need to think about 'How are we as a church speaking harsh words against God?', 'How is our church letting individuals speak harsh words against God and not challenging them?', 'How is my speaking harsh words against God setting a bad example to others in the church?', 'What am I doing to challenge the church as a whole to stop speaking harsh words against God?' and 'What are our church leaders doing to stop individuals and the church speaking harsh words against God?'

However, while the pattern of life of the people of God is Malachi's primary concern, his message is still demanding for individuals!

May God the Holy Spirit write his words through Malachi in our churches, in our hearts, minds, memories, lives and ministries.

---

[1] J. I. Packer, *God Has Spoken* (Grand Rapids: Baker, 1979), p. 97.

Malachi 1:1

1. The word of the Lord

This brief introduction to the book in its first verse tells us four important facts: the book comes from *the* LORD; it is *a prophecy* in the form of *the word*; it is addressed *to Israel*; and it comes *through Malachi*. We need to understand these facts to make the best use of this book, the last of the Old Testament prophets.

1. 'The word of the LORD'

'The LORD' is the God of the Old Testament, the God of the Bible. The Lord who is God 'made the earth and the heavens' (Gen. 2:4), created the man and the woman in the garden near Eden (2:7, 22), judged them for their sin (3:8–24), helped Eve give birth to Cain (4:1), brought the flood to judge the world and saved Noah and his family (6 – 8), scattered the people who were building the tower of Babel (11:1–9), and called Abram to make him a great nation and through him to bless all peoples on earth (12:1–3).

a. Who is this Lord?

'The LORD' is the way our English translations represent the personal name of God. God called Moses, and revealed himself by his personal name, translated in Exodus as 'I am who I am',[1] the covenant name of God:

---

[1] The Hebrew letters for this transliterate into English as YHWH, Yahweh being the modern scholarly rendering.

God said to Moses, 'I AM WHO I AM. This is what you are to say to the
Israelites: "I AM has sent me to you." . . .
  'This is my name for ever,
    the name you shall call me
    from generation to generation.'
(Exod. 3:14–15)

He also proclaimed himself as 'The LORD, the LORD, the compassionate and
gracious God, slow to anger, abounding in love and faithfulness, maintaining
love to thousands . . .' (Exod. 34:6–7)

Three great characteristics of the Lord God in the Old Testament are
that he loves his people, saves his people and speaks to his people.

God's love means that God chose his people, made covenant promises
to his people, fulfilled his covenant and so was faithful to his people. In
his words through Moses,

The LORD did not set his affection on you and choose you because you
were more numerous than other peoples, for you were the fewest of all
peoples. But it was because the LORD loved you and kept the oath he
swore to your ancestors that he brought you out with a mighty hand and
redeemed you from the land of slavery, from the power of Pharaoh king
of Egypt.
(Deut. 7:7–8)

God's love is also seen when God saves or rescues his people when they
have sinned or when they are in danger.

When our ancestors were in Egypt,
    they gave no thought to your miracles;
they did not remember your many kindnesses,
    and they rebelled by the sea, the Red Sea.
Yet he saved them for his name's sake,
    to make his mighty power known.
(Ps. 106:7–8)

Or again, the love of the Lord for his people is celebrated in these words:

The LORD is compassionate and gracious,
    slow to anger, abounding in love.

He will not always accuse,
  nor will he harbour his anger for ever;
he does not treat us as our sins deserve
  or repay us according to our iniquities.
For as high as the heavens are above the earth,
  so great is his love for those who fear him;
as far as the east is from the west,
  so far has he removed our transgressions from us.
(Ps. 103:8–12)

And the Lord's love is seen in his speaking words to his people.

As the rain and the snow
  come down from heaven,
and do not return to it
  without watering the earth
and making it bud and flourish,
  so that it yields seed for the sower and bread for the eater,
so is my word that goes out from my mouth:
  it will not return to me empty,
but will accomplish what I desire,
  and achieve the purpose for which I sent it.
(Isa. 55:10–11)

So God the Lord is one who loves, saves and speaks. And, as these references have made clear, the history of the Lord and his people goes back a long way. These words in Malachi do not initiate a relationship: they come within a long history of God's love for his people, and their response of obedience or disobedience, of faithfulness or unfaithfulness.

God's people in Malachi's day could expect to meet this God in his words through the prophet Malachi. And we should expect to meet this God, our God, who is God the Father, God the Son and God the Spirit, as we read his words through his prophet Malachi.

b. God and our world

In the world in which Malachi wrote his prophecy, most people believed in a god or in gods, and shaped their lives in response to that god or gods. But we read Malachi's words of the Lord in a different world. If we believe in God, it is often in a god who is at the periphery of our lives, not at the centre. Practical atheism or practical agnosticism structures our reality. There are many voices in our world, and we are often deafened to God's voice. We have many responsibilities, and our duty to God is often far down the list. We are busy people, and too busy for God. There is much to read, and God's words are not a priority.

T. E. Lawrence, Lawrence of Arabia, was one of the heroes of the First World War, in which he effectively galvanized the Arabs into rebelling against their Turkish overlords. But his attitude to religion was sadly typical of his day: 'Although brought up in conventional religion, he had long since discarded it, and did not notice the loss.'[2]

And as our culture moves even further from the 'conventional religion' of Christianity, it is harder for us to find room for God in our lives, and so harder for us to find room for the word of the Lord in our lives. Yet even this way of speaking exposes the problem. How dare we think of 'making room' for God the Lord? For the Lord God created and sustains all reality, and holds it together. The real question is this: 'Is there room for us in God's universe?'

And while we may retain a belief in God, it is often God in weakened form, or even belief in godlets, rather than gods, what David Bentley Hart calls 'custom-fitted spiritualities'.[3] Godlets are little gods who can be taken up or put down, adopted for a while as they serve our needs, but then dismissed as they fail us or bore us. People do, as Hart suggests, adopt pagan 'godlets' for as long as they suit them. We may also try to adopt the one Lord God, the true and living God, as a 'godlet', as long as he suits us.

Many common ideas in our world make it difficult for people to receive and believe the Bible and to believe in the one true and living God. Here are some of them:

- *The autonomous individual:* the absolute liberty of personal volition; the self-created person; the right to happiness and personal fulfilment; the danger of repressed desires; the belief that communities are free to make their own rules; the belief that we create ourselves; absolute trust in personal intuition and feelings; absolute trust in 'what everybody thinks'.

---

[2] B. H. L. Hart, *Lawrence of Arabia* (Cambridge: Da Capo Press, 1989 [1937]), p. 367.
[3] D. B. Hart, *In the Aftermath: Provocations and Laments* (Grand Rapids: Eerdmans, 2009), p. 2.

- *Diminished humanity:* belief in various brands of determinism; the view that humans are nothing more than creative animals; the devaluing of humanity and human values; consumerism as a key to personal fulfilment; the belief that human society is predominantly 'an economy', so that politics is economics; the worship of wealth; the worship of celebrities; the simplification of ideas.

- *Diminished or idolatrous view of the universe:* belief in 'Mother Nature' or some other power that controls the universe; profound pessimism about the future; broad trust in progress; trust in Western-developed industrial and scientific capitalism; belief that whatever you happen to believe about what happens to you after death is what will happen to you after death; belief in karma and fate; distrust of meaning in words or texts, or a belief that meaning is the product of the reader's or community's reflections and responses; either believing that only that which is factual, historical and literal has any significance, or else believing that only that which is poetic and non-literal has any significance.[4]

All and each of these will make it hard to believe in one sovereign God. My observation is that people hold their formative ideas at what is commonly called a 'deep' level. That is, they may not be able to articulate them, they may not be able to give reasons for believing them, but they 'know' that they are true. These 'ideas' are deeply held intuitions, most of them received unconsciously from the surrounding culture. They are often strictly speaking 'pre-judices', untested assumptions.

We need to repent of these prejudices, these assumptions, or these commitments, if we are to know the true and living God. May we do so, and so meet God the Lord, revealed through the words of Malachi, and fully revealed in the Lord Jesus Christ, the Word who 'became flesh and made his dwelling among us. We have seen his glory, the glory of the one and only Son . . . full of grace and truth' (John 1:14).

---

[4] See further on these ideas: D. J. Boorstin, *The Image: A Guide to Pseudo-Events in America* (New York: Harper & Row, 1964); M. Robinson, *The Death of Adam: Essays on Modern Thought* (New York: Picador, 2005); *idem, Absence of Mind* (New Haven: Yale University Press, 2010); J. R. Saul, *The Unconscious Civilization* (Ringwood: Penguin, 1997); D. F. Wells, *Above All Earthly Pow'rs: Christ in a Postmodern World* (Grand Rapids: Eerdmans; Nottingham: IVP, 2010).

2. 'A prophecy', 'the word of the LORD'

As we have seen, God the Lord is a God who speaks, and God most often speaks through prophets. Moses was the first prophet, called and commissioned by God, who received words from God that he then passed on to God's people.

a. God's words

There were two kinds of words that Moses received and passed on. The first was the covenant itself, as found in Exodus 20 – 24. This was the covenant statement that was the foundation of God's relationship with his people and of their covenant responsibility, given at Mount Sinai. It included instructions on how they were to behave, and how they were to worship. This was relevant to those who were contemporaries of Moses, and to all subsequent generations. The second was the sermons that Moses preached forty years later, recorded in the book of Deuteronomy, as the people prepared to enter the Promised Land. In these sermons Moses reminded the people of the covenant given at Sinai, applied it to the new situation of God's people, and appealed to the people to respond in faith and obedience. This second kind of message was like that given by later prophets. The message is a reminder of the covenant, an application of it, and an appeal to the people to keep that covenant. As Calvin wrote of Christian preachers, 'we ought to imitate the Prophets, who conveyed the doctrine of the Law in such a manner as to draw from it advices, reproofs, threatenings, and consolations, which they applied to the present condition of the people'.[5]

The word *prophecy* or 'oracle' (NRSV) (*maśśā'*) is linked to the idea of carrying, and is sometimes translated 'burden' (a burden for the prophet and/or for the people). It serves the same purpose as other introductory words for prophecies, such as 'word' and 'vision'. It usually introduces a prophecy about the end times, with a warning of judgment as well as a message of mercy.[6] The book is also described as a *word*, that is, a message. It is the *word of the* LORD. To fail to respond to the word of a prophet is to fail to respond to God:

---

[5] In the preface to his commentary on Isaiah, p. xxx.

[6] It is used ten times in Isa. 13 – 23; to introduce the prophecies of Nahum and Habakkuk; and in Zech. 9:1; 12:1.

Zedekiah was twenty-one years old when he became king, and he reigned in Jerusalem for eleven years. He did evil in the eyes of the LORD his God and did not humble himself before Jeremiah the prophet, who spoke the word of the LORD.
(2 Chr. 36:11–12)

b. Our response

Jeremiah Burroughs was one of the great preachers of the seventeenth century. He wrote a book called *Gospel Worship*, a series of sermons on how to relate to God. He thought that one of the most important things we do each week is to go to church, to listen to the reading and preaching of the Bible. As you sit still to listen, he explains, 'you come to tender up your homage to God, to sit at God's feet and there to profess your submission to Him'.[7]

Isn't it tragic to see married couples when they have stopped listening to each other? Isn't it frustrating to be in a workplace in which people don't listen to one another? Isn't it sad when politicians just repeat their formulas, and don't listen any more? And isn't it distressing when we feel that our friends don't hear what we are saying to them?

All of these things are very sad. But it is even more tragic when God's people don't listen to God's words to them. It is easier to speak than to listen. It is easier to speak to God than it is to listen to God. The words of Malachi were the words of God, for 'no prophecy ever came by human will, but men carried along by the Holy Spirit spoke from God' (2 Pet. 1:21; author's translation). And when the books of the Bible were gathered together, the Bible itself treats the narrative as well as the direct quotations of God's words as the word of God.[8] So the whole of Malachi is the word of God.

Our focus on the Bible is not because of secret bibliolatry, nor because mere Bible knowledge is the heart of Christianity. It is because I want God's voice to be heard, and because I want Christ to be known and trusted. For as John Donne preached, 'The Scriptures are God's voice, the Church is his echo.'[9] And as James Smart wrote, 'Without the Bible the

---

7 J. Burroughs, *Gospel Worship* (Orlando: Soli Deo Gloria, 1990 [1648]), p. 197.

8 P. Adam, *Written for Us: Receiving God's Words in the Bible* (Nottingham: IVP, 2008), pp. 49–52.

9 J. Donne, *The Sermons of John Donne*, vol. 6, eds. M. R. Potter and E. M. Simpson (Berkeley: University of California Press, 1962), p. 223. 'The Scriptures are God's Voyce, the Church is His Echo, a redoubling, a repeating of some particular syllables and accents of the same voice.'

remembered Christ becomes the imagined Christ, [a Christ shaped] by the religiosity and unconscious desires of his worshippers.'[10]

In Deuteronomy 6:4–9 Moses instructed God's people to meditate corporately on the words of God so they might love him. And we must heed the words of Jesus, who warned us that 'If anyone is ashamed of me and my words in this adulterous and sinful generation, the Son of Man will be ashamed of them when he comes in his Father's glory with the holy angels' (Mark 8:38).

Jesus' words are as applicable today as at any time. We must encourage one another to be like the wise person who hears the words of Jesus and does them, not like the foolish person who hears them and does not do them (Matt. 7:24–27). Our lives and ministries will either stand on a firm foundation, or fall with a great crash!

We should recognize the fact that one of the effects of sin is that it blinds us to its presence. If we commit the sin of neglecting, refusing or failing to hear the words of God in Scripture, we will become increasingly blind to the continued presence of that sin, and so complicit in silencing God. We must heed the warning of God to his people: '"When I called, they did not listen; so when they called, I would not listen," says the LORD Almighty' (Zech. 7:13).

Our duty and joy is to hear, receive and obey the words that God has spoken to us in Scripture, so that God might accomplish his good purpose in and through our lives. In the words of Jeremiah Burroughs: 'We should listen as much to the voice of God in the ministry of His Word as if . . . the LORD should speak out of the clouds to us.'[11] In the same way, we should listen to God's words through Malachi.

3. 'To Israel'

These words are remarkable. The people of God, the twelve tribes, were originally one people. They split into two in the time of Jeroboam and Rehoboam, son of Solomon (1 Kgs 12). The northern kingdom (the ten tribes based in Samaria) then became known as Israel, and the southern kingdom (the two tribes based in Jerusalem) were then called Judah. But Israel, the northern kingdom, went into exile under the Assyrians in

---

[10] J. D. Smart, *The Strange Silence of the Bible in the Church* (London: SCM, 1970), p. 25.

[11] Burroughs, *Gospel Worship*, p. 210.

722 BC. It was Judah, the southern kingdom, which went into exile in Babylon and later returned to Jerusalem, which received this prophecy (see the reference to 'the temple' in 1:10, and to 'Judah and Jerusalem' in 3:4).

Why was Judah addressed as *Israel*? The immediate answer is that Malachi is about to refer to the early history of God's people, to Isaac and his two sons Esau and Jacob (Gen. 27 – 35). He will refer to the Lord's love for Jacob, who was later renamed Israel (Gen. 32:28). So he wanted to use the ancient name *Israel* for God's people in his own time. The larger answer is that Judah represents God's people, and inherits all the promises made to all the whole people of God. Or, to put it another way, the northern kingdom, called Israel, has its continued existence in the people of God of Judah in Malachi's day, who are now rightly called *Israel*. And to call Judah *Israel* is also to point to God's fulfilment of his promises to gather his people again into the land and to the city of Jerusalem (see Deut. 30; Ezek. 37; 40 – 48). And we read in 1 Chronicles that some from the northern kingdom did come to settle in Jerusalem after the exile (1 Chr. 9:2–3).

So the people of God were addressed by the name *Israel*, which speaks of God's choice of his people, of his judgment on his people when they turn from him, and also of his effective grace in achieving his long-term saving purpose. For as God is able to make people who are not his people into his people, as he did when he called Abram, and as he did when he forgave people their sin (see Hos. 1:10), so he can make Judah fulfil his promises to the whole people of God, and ultimately bring the nations into the people of God in Christ (see Eph. 2:1 – 3:6).

As we saw in the Introduction, the book of Malachi is addressed to the people of God, the church of his day. It has relevance for individuals, but its primary purpose is to challenge the people of God. It is preaching that aims to change the church, not just change individuals. As that was its original purpose, that is what we should do with it when we preach it today. This way of reading and hearing the Bible also means that you may learn things that you don't need yourself, but which God teaches you so that you will be able to teach, help or train someone else, or answer the questions they ask.

The Bible changes churches, not just individuals. The fruit of the gospel is churches, not just converted individuals. If you want to change a church, then in addition to challenging the church as a whole from the Bible, you also need to challenge the leaders. This is what Malachi does (2:1–9). For where leaders lead, the congregation will follow. The leaders of a church include those who make top-level decisions, those who preach, and those who teach at any level, including small group leaders, youth group leaders, Sunday school teachers and prayer group leaders. It includes those who lead the Sunday services, those who mentor and train others, and those who influence others.

So as we read Malachi, we must work hard to avoid individualizing the message, when it was so clearly and unambiguously addressed by God to Israel, to the church of that day. And we should be working to apply it to the churches to which we belong. Of course we need individuals to be changed by the word of God. But the change that needs to happen to an individual is not just about his or her own personal behaviour: the change that is required is that the individual wants to change the church.

If you are an individual member of a church, then your task is to receive the message of Malachi and think how it applies to your church. Then use the message of Malachi to pray for your church, to encourage your fellow believers, and to help choose leaders for your church. If you are a leader or teacher or mentor in your church, then make sure that you teach and apply the message of Malachi to the people you influence.

4. 'Through Malachi'

So the means that *the* Lord used to bring his *prophecy* (or 'oracle'), his *word* to his people *Israel*, was *Malachi* (1). This is the common pattern in the Old Testament: Moses was the paradigm prophet, for Moses received words from the Lord, then spoke them to the people and wrote them down for the people. These words were written so that there was an authentic record of God's words spoken at that time, and so that later generations could hear and read those words. For Moses 'received living words to pass on to us', in the words of Stephen (Acts 7:38).

Malachi means 'my messenger', which implies 'the Lord's messenger', or God's messenger. As I explained in the Introduction, I think that Malachi was the name of the prophet, and so we should translate Malachi as a name, and not read 1:1 as 'through my messenger'. Malachi prophesied after the return from exile to the people of God in Judah and Jerusalem, when they were under the rule of the Persians. We do not know the exact date, but it was probably between 460 and 400 BC.[12]

---

[12] See Introduction.

Malachi 1:1 asserts that the words of his book are a *prophecy, the word of the* LORD; and that they came *through Malachi.* They are truly *the word of the* LORD, yet they also came *through Malachi.* So we need to accept their divine origin and their human origin, their divine power and their human form, their eternal value and their historical particularity. The divine and human authorship of Malachi and of the other Scriptures provides a fascinating insight into how God achieves his perfect purpose and also respects and uses human agents. Although God is the author of all books of the Bible, he allows each human author to speak and write according to their historical context, in their own language, and in their own personal style. Malachi has his distinctive style, as we will see, and yet also communicates what God intends. What an amazing insight into the gentle but effective power of God, into his respect for humanity, as he achieves his divine purpose. Yet of course we see the same happening in the good works we do. God prepares all our good works, and enables us to do them, yet allows us to do them in ways that fully express our humanity and our personal character and style.

It is not just that God had some general ideas in mind, and then let Malachi use the words that he wanted to use. For this book is *a prophecy,* as well as *the word of the* LORD. Malachi was carried along by the Holy Spirit as he wrote, as we saw above, and the very words he used were inspired by God (2 Pet. 1:21; 2 Tim. 3:16). A 'prophecy' is a complete set of words, a complete text: it is each word as well as the whole message, the words as well as the word.

We should recognize that Old Testament prophets received 'the word' or 'words', or 'vision' or 'oracle' or 'prophecy', in a variety of ways. Some, like Moses, just wrote down and then spoke what they received (Exod. 20 – 24; cf. 24:4). Jonah heard and then rejected what God said, and finally passed it on very reluctantly (Jon. 1:1–10; 3:1–4; 4:1–3). Jeremiah received God's words with delight, but soon wished that he had not been born (Jer. 15:16; 20:14–18). Habakkuk disagreed with God's revealed plan, but finally accepted it (Hab. 1:1 – 2:4; 3:16–19). God called Jeremiah, Ezekiel and Hosea to live their message as well as speak it (Jer. 13:1–11; Ezek. 4 – 5; Hos. 1:1–11).

We do not know what Malachi thought or felt about the oracle that he was called to pass on, but we do know that it was *a prophecy* from God, *the word of the* LORD. For in this matter there is no neutral ground: the words of a prophet are either the words of God, or they are words that come from the imagination of the prophet, which are worthless. God hates being misrepresented, because he values his words and he values his people so much. So God, through Jeremiah, condemned false prophets in these words:

> If a prophet or a priest or anyone else claims, 'This is a message from the LORD,' I will punish them and their household. This is what each of you keeps saying to your friends and other Israelites: 'What is the LORD's answer?' or 'What has the LORD spoken?' But you must not mention 'a message from the LORD' again, because each one's word becomes their own message. So you distort the words of the living God, the LORD Almighty, our God.
> (Jer. 23:34–36)[13]

We may think direct words from God are of more value than words that God speaks through human agents, and especially from humans who lived so long ago! The Reformer John Calvin described God's use of human mouthpieces in these words:

> But as God did not entrust the ancient folk to angels but raised up teachers from the earth truly to perform the angelic office, so also today it is his will to teach us through human means. As he was of old not content with the law alone, but added priests as interpreters from whose lips the people might ask its true meaning, so today he not only desires us to be attentive to its reading but also appoints instructors to help us by their effort. This is doubly useful. On the one hand, he provokes our obedience by a very good test when we hear his ministers speaking just as if he himself spoke. On the other hand, he also provides for our weakness in that he prefers to address us in human fashion through interpreters in order to draw us to himself, rather than to thunder at us and drive us away.[14]

We might think that while we must obey words that come directly from the mouth of God, we can afford to give less attention to words that he sends us through the minds and mouths of his human agents. This would be a great mistake. For, as Amos said: 'Surely the Sovereign LORD does

---

13 The NIV translates 'oracle' as 'message' in this passage.
14 Calvin, *Institutes*, 4.1.5.

nothing without revealing his plan to his servants the prophets' (Amos 3:7). And Jesus told his messengers: 'Whoever listens to you listens to me; whoever rejects you rejects me; but whoever rejects me rejects him who sent me' (Luke 10:16).

5. Our response

What then should we do in response to *A prophecy: the word of the* Lord *to Israel through Malachi*?

We should listen to, receive or welcome Malachi and his words, knowing that when we do this we listen to the voice of God. We should expect that we will be made wise for salvation through faith in Christ Jesus, and also be thoroughly equipped for every good work (see 2 Tim. 3:15–17).

We should heed the words of the Lord Jesus: 'How foolish you are, and how slow to believe all that the prophets have spoken!', and we should avoid this rebuke. Rather we should search out 'everything [that] must be fulfilled' about Christ 'written . . . in the Law of Moses, the Prophets and the Psalms' (Luke 24:25, 44).

We should receive these words from the Old Testament as the present words of the Holy Spirit: 'as the Holy Spirit says' (Heb. 3:7), as 'living words' (Acts 7:38) handed down for us. Above all, we should love God fully and completely by receiving his words, meditating on them, and encouraging one another with them. For the great paradigm of the relationship between the people of God and the words of God is found in Deuteronomy 6. Here God through Moses told his people to love him: 'Hear, O Israel: the Lord our God, the Lord is one. Love the Lord your God with all your heart and with all your soul and with all your strength' (Deut. 6:4–5). And then God through Moses told them how they should love him:

These commandments that I give you today are to be on your hearts. Impress them on your children. Talk about them when you sit at home and when you walk along the road, when you lie down and when you get up. Tie them as symbols on your hands and bind them on your foreheads. Write them on the door-frames of your houses and on your gates.
(Deut. 6:6–9)

And yet, as Jeremiah prophesied (Jer. 7:23–26), God's people habitually refused to receive God's words through his prophets. This sin had led to the exile. What will the people of God do now, when the word of the Lord comes by Malachi?

When we read a book like Malachi, we experience increasing tension. For yet again God is speaking to his people through his prophet; once again, God's words come to God's people. And what will happen this time? Will they respond with faith, obedience and praise, or will they harden their hearts and stop their ears against the gracious words of God? Will they let God speak, or will they silence him?

The same issue confronts us about our churches today. It is not enough for some people in the church to be committed to reading the Bible, and not enough for the preacher to be committed to preaching the Scriptures. Will the people of God welcome the words of God today? Will they love God by loving his words? Will they follow the ancient advice of King Jehoshaphat: 'Listen to me, Judah and people of Jerusalem! Have faith in the LORD your God and you will be upheld; have faith in his prophets and you will be successful' (2 Chr. 20:20).

This is a vital issue for the church of God in every age: will we receive the words of God in Scripture? It is an issue for every church, just as it is an issue for every preacher and an issue for every Christian. Listen to the response of the great English Reformer Thomas Cranmer: 'My very foundation is only upon God's Word, which foundation is so sure that it never will fail.'[15] And Cranmer warns us:

> If there were any word of God beside the Scripture, we could never be certain of God's Word; and if we be uncertain of God's Word the devil might bring in among us a new word, a new doctrine, a new faith, a new church, a new God, or even himself to be god . . . If the Church and the Christian faith did not stay itself upon the word of God certain, as upon a sure and strong foundation, no man could know where he had the right faith, and whether he were in the true Church of Christ, or in the synagogue of Satan.[16]

As we read Malachi, may we receive these precious words of God. May we be encouraged by other believers who have welcomed God's messengers, like the Thessalonians who welcomed Paul's gospel words:

---

[15] T. Cranmer, *Works of Thomas Cranmer: Writing and Disputations of Thomas Cranmer . . . Relative to the Sacrament of the Lord's Supper*, ed. J. E. Cox, The Parker Society (Cambridge: Cambridge University Press, 1844), vol. 1, p. 255.

[16] T. Cranmer, *Confutation*, as quoted in P. E. Hughes, *Theology of the English Reformers* (London: Hodder & Stoughton, 1965), pp. 31–32.

And we also thank God continually because, when you received the word of God, which you heard from us, you accepted it not as a human word, but as it actually is, the word of God, which is indeed at work in you who believe.
(1 Thess. 2:13)

Hear the word of the Lord; thanks be to God.

Malachi 1:2–5

2. I have loved you

1. I have loved you (1:2)

What a striking start to this oracle! *'I have loved you,' says the Lord* (2) sets the tone of the book, gives reassurance and challenge, and places at the centre of the book the issue of what God has done and what God has revealed. The book does not start with a summary of what the people have done or not done, but what God has done. It does not start with what the people have done to God, but what God has done to the people. He has loved them.

What a frightening start to this oracle! For the Lord expresses his love and action, *I have loved you*, but immediately follows this with the instinctive contradictory response of the people that is deep within their hearts, minds, lives and lips: *How have you loved us?* To deny that God has loved them is to deny God. This contradiction of God lies deep in the hearts of the people.

And it is not only that this response was instinctive and characteristic, as we have seen, it is also that in the structure of Malachi's prophecy the first sin named, that of doubting God's love, naturally led to the other sins. They are in that grey 'no-man's land', that imagined neutral territory, with neither the courage to respond wholeheartedly to God, nor the courage to refuse him.

Contradicting God and his words was unfortunately characteristic of this contrary people. Whatever God said, they contradicted by similar questions (as we saw in the Introduction), when they should have known that God loved them. It was clearly taught in their Scriptures, and evident in all the signs of God's effective electing love, not least in bringing them back from exile in Babylon, in the rebuilding of Jerusalem and of the temple, and in the continued provision of priest, sacrifices and prophets.

The people are on a downward spiral away from God, and will grow ever more bitter and cynical and negative, unless God miraculously recalls them to repentance and restores them by this prophetic word. They are in a vicious cycle, a terrifying whirlpool, sinking further and further towards destruction. Because they don't know God's covenant love, they despise God, despise the atonement he provides, break covenant faith, become cynical about God's promises, show reluctant obedience, show active disobedience, and face God's judgment.

They would not have existed as God's people unless God had loved them, had chosen them in their ancestors (in Abraham, Isaac and Jacob) and had maintained his constant faithful covenant love by forgiving their sins and rebellions, restoring them when they were in trouble, rescuing them from their enemies, providing for their needs, answering their prayers, providing them with priests and sacrifices for atonement, and sending prophets, wise men and wise women, to teach and encourage them. To deny that God loved them was to deny God, and to deny the grace of God in making them his people, to deny their own identity as God's flock, nation and people, and to deny their special calling to bring blessing to all the nations of the world.

Furthermore, their contradiction of God is fundamental to their lives and is fully expressed in their words: *But you ask, 'How have you loved us?'* Their refusal to accept God's love is expressed not just in their inner thoughts, or in their actions, but in their words. This means that they are constantly spreading this contagion among themselves, constantly reinforcing this attitude, and encouraging one another to doubt God's love. *How have you loved us?* exposes deep and dangerous sins, and the vast gap that exists between God and his covenant people. What is on their lips comes from what is in their hearts, for 'the mouth speaks what the heart is full of' (Matt. 12:34).

We human beings are incurably self-centred and self-focused. Augustine of Hippo thought that self-love was the great enemy of love of God, and Martin Luther described us as 'curved in on ourselves'. Our first questions are 'How am I?', 'How are we?' And these questions blind us to who God is, what God thinks, how God feels, what God has said, what God has done. This is why the first words of the prophecy are about God, what God has felt, done and said. How amazing it is that when we are asked how we are, we naturally answer in terms of human well-being, health, happiness, human relationships, contentment, wealth and the welfare of our environment and society. We neglect the biggest issue, which is how we are with God, and the most important aspect of that issue, which is not what we feel about God, but what God feels about us. How amazing that though we know we are not the centre of the universe, we feel, think, relate and act as if we are. Our self-centredness blinds us to God; we try to live in a fool's paradise, when in fact it is more like hell than a paradise. 'God last' rather than 'God first' is our effective motto and rule.

If humans as individuals function this way, then so do churches, so do communities and so do nations. Malachi's focus is of course the people of God, the church-nation of his day. If it is frightening to find a selfish Christian, it is even more frightening to find a selfish church. And while selfishness that ignores other people is damaging, selfishness that ignores God is damnable. A self-centred church will be a selfish church. It will have its own comfort and convenience as its aim, and its own happiness and satisfaction as its guide. It will not convert unbelievers, care for the needy, serve its community or raise up gospel workers for the world. It will not have the glory, honour and gospel plan of God as its main priority. Its selfish life will betray its selfish heart. Its selfish actions will betray its selfish instincts.

As all reputable crime writers point out, murdering someone not only damages the person who is dead, but also damages the murderer. One of the frightening consequences of any sin is that it blinds us not only to the reality of specific sins we have committed, but also to all sin. What great sins the people must have committed to make this response: *How have you loved us?* They are really saying, 'Prove it': challenging God to show them his love, and so negating all that God has done and said to them over past generations, and in their own experience.

It is such a distancing and defeating response, the kind of response that could easily kill a marriage or end a friendship. It is defeating because it undermines not only the present words of God, *I have loved you*, but also all that God has been in his covenant love in all generations, and his constant love to his people at that time.

What a frightening example of how sin blinds and binds, as we will know in our own lives and in the lives of our churches. For every time we sin, that sin makes us blind to its presence, less able to see it, and so more likely to repeat it. And sin binds, because every time we sin we weaken our power to resist sinning, and take the first steps in forming the habit of repeating that sin. As has often been said:[1] 'Sow a thought, and you reap an act. Sow an act, and you reap a habit. Sow a habit, and you reap a character. Sow a character, and you reap a destiny.'

The people of God in Malachi's day are so blind to their sin: *'I have loved you,' says the* LORD. *'But you ask, "How have you loved us?"'* Nowadays, we might say that they lack emotional intelligence. Emotional intelligence includes awareness of oneself and one's emotions, and awareness of others and their emotions. But they are blind to the love of God.

Have you ever noticed those sins in the lives of others which they don't recognize but which are so obvious to everyone else? It really is bizarre how blind other people can be to their obvious sins. Have you ever wondered if perhaps you have sins like that? Your friends and family know all about them, but you just don't see them. Has it struck you that if everyone else has these sins which they don't recognize, that you might have them as well?

This simple truth struck me just five years ago, and I began praying each day that God would show me my secret sins – I mean secret to me, though not secret to God or to others! God is slowly showing me these sins, and enabling me to repent; I am sure that there are many more to come.

But if our sins blind us to their presence in us as individuals, then of course the sins of churches also blind the members of those churches to their presence. What might some of these sins be? No doubt God will show them to us, and I pray that God would use Malachi to make our hidden sins plain. We must pray that God would cleanse us from these secret sins by showing them to us by his Spirit, by enabling our repentance, by cleansing us by the blood of the Lord Jesus and the power of his atoning death, and by enabling us to die to sin and to live to righteousness.

The great sin of God's people in the Old Testament had been idolatry, the turning to other gods and so turning away from their own God, the Lord. The sin of idolatry was there when the people made a golden calf to worship at Mount Sinai. It was the sin of idolatry that led to the destruction of the northern kingdom of Israel and their exile in Assyria, and to the exile of the southern kingdom in Babylon (Exod. 32:1–35; 2 Kgs 17:7–23; Ezek. 16). It seems as if the exile did heal God's people of the grossest idolatry. Unfortunately, here in Malachi, we find that they have

---

[1] Anonymously, although it has been attributed to a number of different people.

found an alternative sin. If they could not turn to other gods, then they could still keep their God at a distance, they could doubt his love, his deeds and his words. Perhaps they were not brave enough to say that God did not love them: they were just brave enough to ask the damaging and revealing question, *How have you loved us?*

We call this 'sulking' and it is very tiresome and very destructive. It is common in marriages, in families, among adolescents, among adults, among the elderly, in churches and in society in general. In its worst form, its weapon is refusal to speak or to meet. But the form we see here in Malachi is distressing enough. Here it is the power play of implied contradiction, requiring the other person to meet your needs, to meet your standards, to work harder, to prove what he or she says. It is the response of distrust, of lack of positive engagement, a self-imposed refusal to give a positive reaction or comment.

It looks as if God's people think that they have found a satisfactory neutral middle ground between obedience and disobedience. They will not obey God, nor do they have the nerve to disobey him. They think they can remain God's people, questioning and criticizing him, distrusting him and declining to obey him. But there is no neutral ground. Malachi in the Old Testament, like Paul in the New, was an ambassador, calling on God's people to be reconciled to God, exhorting them not to receive the grace of God in vain (2 Cor. 5:18 – 6:2).

They were in a state of mind that is very common for churches and Christians today: not brave enough to turn away from God, but not brave enough to love and serve him wholeheartedly. We imagine that we can live in a neutral zone, and avoid decisive action. But there is no neutral zone. If we are not building our marriages year by year, then they are fraying. If we are not growing in our trust in God, then that trust is shrinking. If we are not dying to sin, then sin is growing in power. If we are not living in righteousness, then we are walking away from it. If we are not keeping in step with the Spirit, then we are walking to a different drumbeat, our own selfish desires. If the fruit of the Spirit is not increasing in our lives, then the works of the flesh will be gaining in power over us.

Rather than asking, *How have you loved us?*, they should have known that, in the words of God through Jeremiah, 'I have loved you with an everlasting love; I have drawn you with unfailing kindness' (Jer. 31:3). They should have celebrated, in the words of Lamentations, that

Because of the LORD's great love we are not consumed,
    for his compassions never fail.
They are new every morning;
    great is your faithfulness.
(Lam. 3:22–23)

They should have joined in Psalm 136, with its rousing refrain 'His love endures for ever.' But instead of praising God for his steadfast love, they are asking the miserable and miserly question *How have you loved us?*

However, we should not think that it is always wrong to ask this question. It is not that God's people must refuse to face the difficult questions of the life of faith, and nor are they required to ignore their feelings. There are plenty of examples in the Psalms of the saints questioning God, and looking for reassurance and answers to their questions from within difficult situations. The healthy reaction to such situations is to face the question, and to persist in bringing our grief, complaints, questions or laments to God. We should then wait on God and search the Scriptures for his response. We will find this response as we remember God's words and God's works, ponder the character of God, realize the greatness of God, and look to God for positive steps to take to find resolution.

Frequently in the Psalms the question is, 'You have loved us in the past; where is your love today?' (see e.g. Ps. 89). Here in Malachi's day there was a different situation. Here God's people had drifted into or embraced a settled, consistent and shared attitude of distancing God. They did this by speaking, living and acting as if their needs were of central importance and as if God had let them down, so they thought that cynicism rather than faith and obedience were justified. Their attitude was, 'Let's get away with the least possible response to God', rather than obeying the Shema: 'Hear, O Israel: the LORD our God, the LORD is one. Love the LORD your God with all your heart and with all your soul and with all your strength' (Deut. 6:4–5). They engaged in public denigration of God, rather than praising him for his steadfast love. They were very far away from Psalm 145:4: 'One generation commends your works to another; they tell of your mighty acts.'

The student evangelist Howard Guinness had this advice for young Christians: 'Live dangerously, love lavishly, serve humbly.'[2] We certainly

---

[2] Quoted in an address to mark the 75th anniversary of Melbourne University Christian Union in 2005.

will not live this way if we doubt and disbelieve God's great covenant love for us, his people.

All this is very alarming. What is even more disturbing is that it is clear that here, as so often in the Bible, the sin is a corporate sin, not a personal sin. *They* are saying, *How have you loved us?*, and no-one seems to be questioning that contradiction of God. It is not until Malachi 3:16 that we meet those who have been moved by God's words to change their ways. It had become socially acceptable among the people of God to question God.

What might that look like today? Those who might think that it was wrong to question God's love would face social pressures to conform; young people would grow up to think that this was the normal way to treat God, rather than praising him for his love; the leaders of the community would fail to rebuke this behaviour; every time someone expressed doubt of God's love in public it would reinforce this behaviour; and this shared sin would blind everyone to its presence. Corporate, shared sins are more pernicious than private sins because they are publicly acceptable, and every time they are committed they reinforce bad behaviour, and make it more difficult for an individual to avoid committing the same sin. As there is nothing more helpful to the individual than corporate righteousness, so there is nothing more damaging to the individual than corporate sin. This is painfully evident in Malachi, as it is painfully evident throughout the Bible.

So too in our churches, shared sins are the most sinful ones, because they ensnare us all, cause the weak to stumble, and mislead new and young believers. Fortunately the Bible shows us how to deal with shared corporate sins, as it shows us how to encourage shared corporate righteousness and goodness, because it is the shared life of the people of God that is the Bible's main concern. And this was the work of Christ our Saviour, who died for his bride, the church:

> Christ loved the church and gave himself up for her to make her holy,
> cleansing her by the washing with water through the word, and to
> present her to himself as a radiant church, without stain or wrinkle
> or any other blemish, but holy and blameless.
> (Eph. 5:25–27)

2. I have loved Jacob but hated Esau (1:2–5)

How does God reply to the question *How have you loved us?* The answer is God's electing love, his free choice out of Isaac and Rebekah's twin sons of the younger brother Jacob over his older twin Esau. *'Was not Esau Jacob's brother?' declares the LORD. 'Yet I have loved Jacob, but Esau I have hated'* (2–3). When they were in Rebekah's womb, the Lord told her,

> Two nations are in your womb,
>   and two peoples from within you will be separated;
> one people will be stronger than the other,
>   and the elder will serve the younger.
> (Gen. 25:23)

We see the result of God's choice of Jacob and not Esau in the fact that Esau willingly sold his birthright to Jacob for a meal, thus despising that birthright (Gen. 25:29–34; Heb. 12:16–17). We see it in Rebekah and Jacob's effective deceit of blind Isaac, so that Isaac blessed Jacob with the blessing he intended for Esau, his older son and his favourite (Gen. 27:1–40). We see it in the trials, prosperity and humbling of Jacob, chosen and loved by God despite his many sins and weaknesses (Gen. 28 – 33). We also see it worked out in the many times in which the Edomites, Esau's descendants, persecuted the people of God (Num. 20:14–21; Jer. 49:7–22; Ezek. 25:12–14; Obad.). So in God's words to the Edomites through Ezekiel:

> This is what the Sovereign LORD says: 'Because Edom took revenge on Judah and became very guilty by doing so, therefore this is what the Sovereign LORD says: I will stretch out my hand against Edom and kill both man and beast. I will lay it waste, and from Teman to Dedan they will fall by the sword.'
> (Ezek. 25:12–13)

Edom was oppressed by Babylon in the same way as was Judah (Jer. 25:21; 27:1–11). However, Edom was not the object of God's electing love, unlike the descendants of Jacob/Israel. Though the earthly destinies of the two nations appeared to be very similar, a vast gulf separated them. Both were descendants of Abraham, but Israel was chosen by God, and Edom was not. Both Israel and Edom deserved God's wrath and judgment.

Indeed, Israel perhaps deserved even more wrath and judgment, because of its greater privileges; for greater blessing brings greater responsibility and so greater judgment (see Heb. 10:26–31). Both were under God's wrath and hatred because of their sin; but in Israel's case God covered his wrath with his mercy, and in Edom's case he did not. It was not that Jacob deserved better treatment than Esau, or that God's people deserved better treatment than the Edomites. It was the case that God had decided to set his love on undeserving Israel, and to continue that covenant love to his own people. An outsider might see very little difference between Israel and Edom, but those who have heard the word of God know that there is a great difference between them. As John Calvin wrote in his commentary on Malachi:

> when God visits sins in common (that is, common to the elect and those who are not elect), he ever moderates his wrath towards his elect, and sets limits to his severity, according to what he says, 'If his posterity keep not my covenant, but profane my law, I will chastise them with the rod of man; but my mercy I will not take away from him' (Psalm 89:31–33; 2 Samuel 7:14).[3]

We see here the historical working out of the practical implications of God's election of Israel, and the fact that he did not choose Edom. Despite Israel's sin, God did not remove his long-term plan to bless his people and to bless all the nations through Israel's Messiah. God had no such plan for Edom. So whereas Israel is called 'the holy land',[4] Edom is here called *the Wicked Land* (4).

Both Israel and Edom rebuilt after destruction, but whereas Israel's rebuilding was a sign of eternal hope, no such promise was attached for Edom. It is not clear what specific historical situation is being referred to in these verses. Edom was finally destroyed by the Nabateans in 312 BC, well after this prophecy. They were replaced by the Idumeans, made up of a mixture of Nabateans and Edomites. We read of Idumeans coming to hear Jesus teach in Mark 3:8, with a new opportunity to turn to God in faith and repentance.

You might think that Israel did not actually fare much better. After all, Israel was captured by the Greeks in 332 BC, then, after a brief time of

---

3 Calvin, commentary on Mal. 1:2–6 in *Malachi*, p. 469.
4 'The LORD will inherit Judah as his portion in the holy land and will again choose Jerusalem' (Zech. 2:12).

independence, captured by the Romans in 63 BC. Jerusalem and its temple were later destroyed by the Romans, and the Jewish people thrown out of the land in AD 135. Yet, of course, God continued his electing love for his people, in the Jews and Gentiles who became the church of Jesus Christ (see Rom. 9 – 11; Eph. 2:1 – 3:6).

So the relative historical situations of Israel and Edom were a sign of a greater and eternal destiny. For as we see in Hebrews 11, believers in the Old Testament knew that the land pointed to a reality and a future beyond itself.

> By faith Abraham, when called to go to a place he would later receive as his inheritance, obeyed and went, even though he did not know where he was going. By faith he made his home in the promised land like a stranger in a foreign country; he lived in tents, as did Isaac and Jacob, who were heirs with him of the same promise. For he was looking forward to the city with foundations, whose architect and builder is God . . . All these people were still living by faith when they died. They did not receive the things promised; they only saw them and welcomed them from a distance. . . Therefore God is not ashamed to be called their God, for he has prepared a city for them.
>
> (Heb. 11:8–10, 13, 16)

The real point is not how long God's people lived in the land, but how their eternal destiny is reflected in their historical situation. Israel's return from exile in Babylon was a sign of God's eternal purpose and plan. What happens to Edom will reflect its eternal destiny as well. For God will judge Edom by sending disaster, and though they plan to rebuild, they will fail. They may say, *Though we have been crushed, we will rebuild the ruins*, but *the LORD Almighty says: 'They may build, but I will demolish'* (4). For ultimately humans cannot defeat God's plans, nor escape God's judgment.

Is it right for God to judge Edom? Yes, because they are characterized by wickedness: they are *the Wicked Land*. Was not Israel wicked as well? Yes, but God has had mercy on Israel, and so the holy God has made his people holy. God is free to act in mercy, and free to give mercy to those whom he chooses. This destruction of Edom will be a sign of hope for Israel: *You will see it with your own eyes and say, 'Great is the LORD – even beyond the borders of Israel!'* (5).

It is not that Israel is safe from attack and defeat; it is in the historical defeat of Edom that Israel, taught by God through his prophets, will see a sign of hope, a reminder of God's mercy on them, and a sign of the future judgment. For the Lord is not just a local God. He is the judge of all the earth and all the nations; he is great *beyond* and above *the borders of Israel.* And Israel's continued existence (*you will see it with your own eyes*) is a reminder of God's grace and love in making them his holy people.

All this shows that God's word is true: *I have loved you* (2). God's people should know that they are loved by God; individual believers should know that God loves his people; and the world should know that God loves his people. And the convincing sign of God's love is that he has not dealt with us according to our sins but according to his mercy; that in his wrath he has remembered his mercy (Ps. 103:10; Hab. 3:2). The only escape from the wrath of the Lamb is to find our refuge in the blood of the slaughtered Lamb: 'because you were slain, and with your blood you purchased for God persons from every tribe and language and people and nation' (Rev. 5:9).

And the church today, like the church in Malachi's day, is saved only by God's mercy.

At one time we too were foolish, disobedient, deceived and enslaved by all kinds of passions and pleasures. We lived in malice and envy, being hated and hating one another. But when the kindness and love of God our Saviour appeared, he saved us, not because of righteous things we had done, but because of his mercy. He saved us through the washing of rebirth and renewal by the Holy Spirit, whom he poured out on us generously through Jesus Christ our Saviour, so that, having been justified by his grace, we might become heirs having the hope of eternal life.
(Titus 3:3–7)

Do we find this language of love and hate hard to accept? Remember that Jesus used this language in a similar way when he said, 'If anyone comes to me and does not hate father and mother, wife and children, brothers and sisters – yes, even their own life – such a person cannot be my disciple' (Luke 14:26). And the fact of God's electing love was also seen in the ministry of Jesus, as he himself observed in his thanksgiving to God:

I praise you, Father, Lord of heaven and earth, because you have hidden these things from the wise and learned, and revealed them to little children. Yes, Father, for this is what you were pleased to do.

All things have been committed to me by my Father. No one knows the Son except the Father, and no one knows the Father except the Son and those to whom the Son chooses to reveal him.
(Matt. 11:25–27)

Paul developed these same ideas in Romans, as he commented on the same story of Jacob and Esau.

It is not as though God's word had failed. For not all who are descended from Israel are Israel. Nor because they are his descendants are they all Abraham's children. On the contrary, 'It is through Isaac that your offspring will be reckoned.' In other words, it is not the children by physical descent who are God's children, but it is the children of the promise who are regarded as Abraham's offspring . . .

Not only that, but Rebekah's children were conceived at the same time by our father Isaac. Yet, before the twins were born or had done anything good or bad – in order that God's purpose in election might stand: not by works but by him who calls – she was told, 'The older will serve the younger.' Just as it is written: 'Jacob I loved, but Esau I hated.'

What then shall we say? Is God unjust? Not at all! For he says to Moses, 'I will have mercy on whom I have mercy,
and I will have compassion on whom I have compassion.'
(Rom. 9:6–15)

This is no harsher than Jesus' words to his disciples:

The secret of the kingdom of God has been given to you. But to those on the outside everything is said in parables so that,
'they may be ever seeing but never perceiving,
and ever hearing but never understanding;
otherwise they might turn and be forgiven!'
(Mark 4:11–12, with its quotation of Isa. 6:9–10)

This is just the consequence of the general principle that Paul explains in Ephesians:

For it is by grace you have been saved, through faith – and this is not from yourselves, it is the gift of God – not by works, so that no one can boast. For we are God's handiwork, created in Christ Jesus to do good works, which God prepared in advance for us to do.
(Eph. 2:8–10)

Does God love the church? Does God love me? If we try to answer these questions in terms of how we feel, or in terms of how blessed we are in the way that God has met our needs or desires, or in terms of comparing ourselves with others, we may at times doubt God's love. The overwhelming and convincing proof of God's love is that he has not dealt with us as our sins deserve, but has had mercy on us in Christ Jesus and his atoning death. So through the sacrifice of Christ he has set the judgment and wrath that we deserve aside from us, and has clothed us in Christ's righteousness. He has not reckoned our sins against us, but accepts us in his beloved Son: as Christ took our sins, so we receive his righteousness. This is God's amazing grace to his people in general and to each one of them individually. This is the convincing sign of God's love. We think that we will make God appear more loving by setting aside his wrath and judgment; in fact if we do this we obscure God's love, and make ourselves depend on our feelings and circumstances, and so more vulnerable to doubts and despair. 'I have loved you,' says the LORD. 'But you ask, "How have you loved us?" Was not Esau Jacob's brother?' declares the LORD. 'Yet I have loved Jacob, but Esau I have hated' (2–3).

If we assess God's love by how he meets our needs, then our greedy hearts will always find him wanting. If we assess God's love by his mercy in saving us from the death, judgment and hell that we by nature and by actions deserve, then we will constantly marvel at his amazing love and amazing grace.

This is a really important issue for us as we think about the meaning of the death of Christ. We often think of Christ as saving us from needs and problems that are central to our own concerns. We praise Christ that he has saved us from failure, futility, loneliness, lack of meaning or lack of joy. We praise Christ that he has loved us, and revealed the love of God. However, we easily miss the main point of our salvation: Christ has saved us from God's just judgment, from his wrath and condemnation. For 'God was reconciling the world to himself in Christ, not counting people's sins against them . . . God made him who had no sin to be

sin for us, so that in him we might become the righteousness of God'
(2 Cor. 5:19, 21).

How does Christ show us the love of God? The answer of the New Testament is that Christ shows us God's love, and God shows us his love in
Christ, in that Christ came for unworthy people, God's enemies, ungodly
sinners dead in our sins, and that Christ laid down his life as a sacrifice,
and rose again to make us alive with him.

For God so loved the world that he gave his one and only Son, that
whoever believes in him shall not perish but have eternal life.
(John 3:16)

This is love: not that we loved God, but that he loved us and sent his Son
as an atoning sacrifice for our sins.
(1 John 4:10)

You see, at just the right time, when we were still powerless, Christ died
for the ungodly. Very rarely will anyone die for a righteous person,
though for a good person someone might possibly dare to die. But God
demonstrates his own love for us in this: while we were still sinners,
Christ died for us.
    Since we have now been justified by his blood, how much more
shall we be saved from God's wrath through him! For if, while we were
God's enemies, we were reconciled to him through the death of his Son,
how much more, having been reconciled, shall we be saved through
his life!
(Rom. 5:6–10)

But because of his great love for us, God, who is rich in mercy, made us
alive with Christ even when we were dead in transgressions – it is by
grace you have been saved. And God raised us up with Christ and seated
us with him in the heavenly realms in Christ Jesus, in order that in the
coming ages he might show the incomparable riches of his grace,
expressed in his kindness to us in Christ Jesus.
(Eph. 2:4–7)

If God is for us, who can be against us? He who did not spare his own
Son, but gave him up for us all – how will he not also, along with him,

graciously give us all things? Who will bring any charge against those whom God has chosen? It is God who justifies. Who then is the one who condemns? No one. Christ Jesus who died – more than that, who was raised to life – is at the right hand of God and is also interceding for us . . . For I am convinced that [nothing] will be able to separate us from the love of God that is in Christ Jesus our Lord.
(Rom. 8:31–34, 38–39)

The point is underlined by the challenge to love our enemies, as God loved us, his enemies (Matt. 5:43–47; Rom. 5:6–11; 12:17–21).

If we do not know the wrath of God, we will not know the love of God. The more we understand his wrath, the more we will marvel at his merciful love, his grace to us in his Son. Perhaps our failure to know the length, breadth, height and depth of God's love in Christ[5] comes from our lack of love for God. If the people of God in Malachi's day had loved God more enthusiastically and wholeheartedly, they would have increased their awareness of God's love for them. As C. S. Lewis observed:

> Indeed, if we consider the unblushing promises of reward and the staggering nature of the rewards promised in the Gospels, it would seem that Our Lord finds our desires, not too strong, but too weak. We are half-hearted creatures, fooling about with drink and sex and ambition when infinite joy is offered to us, like an ignorant child who wants to go on making mud pies in a slum because he cannot imagine what is meant by the offer of a holiday at sea. We are far too easily pleased.[6]

Or perhaps we look to our daily lives for convincing evidence of God's love, and find that he has failed, because he has not treated us as well as we deserve. We should then remind ourselves of words attributed to Leighton Ford: 'God loves us the way we are, but too much to leave us that way.'

Where did God want his people to be? He wanted them to know his love, so that they would test his good promises, receive his blessings, and so know his love.

---

[5] Using words from Eph. 3:18.
[6] C. S. Lewis, *The Weight of Glory and Other Addresses* (Grand Rapids: Eerdmans, 1974), pp. 1–2.

John Newton's words are sung around the world: 'Amazing grace! . . . that saved a wretch like me!' Praise God that we can sing those words too today. We could also sing, 'Amazing grace, that saved a church like us!'

Praise God for his honest words of truth to his people. May we hear and receive them deeply today.

Malachi 1:6–14

3. Don't despise me

1. Despising God's name (1:6–9)

What is the first sign of failing to praise God for his covenant love? What is one of the symptoms of this deep disease? Despising God's name. And what is the practical action that shows that God's people are despising God's name? Offering polluted food on God's altar.

The prophet shows the painful contrast between the shared common values demonstrated in their society – *A son honours his father, and a slave his master* – and their shared common way of treating God: *If I am a father, where is the honour due to me? If I am a master, where is the respect due to me?* (6). You might have thought that in a society where sons generally honour fathers and servants generally honour masters then God's people would automatically honour God – that indeed they would be likely to give God even greater honour. But the way they treat one another is in strongest contrast to the way they treat God. They do not honour God, they dishonour him; they hold him up to public disgrace.

The priests should have taken note of the history recorded in Leviticus of the sin of Nadab and Abihu:

> Aaron's sons Nadab and Abihu took their censers, put fire in them and added incense; and they offered unauthorised fire before the LORD, contrary to his command. So fire came out from the presence of the LORD and consumed them, and they died before the LORD. Moses then said to Aaron, 'This is what the LORD spoke of when he said,
> ' "Among those who approach me
>   I will be proved holy;

in the sight of all the people
I will be honoured."'
(Lev. 10:1–3)

The sin, according to God, is that the priests *show contempt for my name* (6). What is it to show contempt towards, or to despise, God's name? It is much more than what we think of as taking God's name in vain, the careless use of God's name in common speech. The name of God in the Bible means the revealed character of God and the presence of God, for when the Lord appeared to Moses, he proclaimed his name, as we have seen:

> Then the LORD came down in the cloud and stood there with him and proclaimed his name, the LORD. And he passed in front of Moses, proclaiming, 'The LORD, the LORD, the compassionate and gracious God, slow to anger, abounding in love and faithfulness, maintaining love to thousands . . .'
> (Exod. 34:5–7)

So to despise or show contempt for God's name is to despise who God is, to despise the self-revelation of God, the character of God. And to despise God's name is also to despise the presence of God, since God 'makes his name dwell' in the temple.

When King Solomon was dedicating the first temple, he prayed,

> But will God really dwell on earth? The heavens, even the highest heaven, cannot contain you. How much less this temple I have built! Yet give attention to your servant's prayer and his plea for mercy, LORD my God. Hear the cry and the prayer that your servant is praying in your presence this day. May your eyes be open towards this temple night and day, this place of which you said, 'My Name shall be there', so that you will hear the prayer your servant prays towards this place.
> (1 Kgs 8:27–29)[1]

---

[1] See also the references to the name of God later in this chapter, e.g. vv. 42–48. This first temple was destroyed by the Babylonians. The temple referred to in Malachi was the second temple on the same site in Jerusalem, built after the return from exile in Babylon. The temple referred to in the New Testament was King Herod's massive rebuild, the third temple on that site, and one of the wonders of the ancient world.

So it is not as if God is a long distance away. He has made himself present in the temple, he has made himself accessible to them; yet even when he is present, they despise him. As Gordon Wenham comments on sacrifices: 'The aim of these rituals is to make possible God's continued presence among his people',[2] just as these rituals also made it possible for the people to stand before their God. God was present, and their indifference to his presence increased the severity of their sin.

God's name is a central theme in Malachi. God's priests despise God's name (6), though God's name will be great among the nations, and will be feared among the nations (11, 14). The priests should 'resolve to honour' God's name (2:2), and follow the example of Levi the priest, who 'revered me and stood in awe of my name' (2:5). For, as we have seen, God's name is his revealed character and his presence among his people in the temple. Later we read of 'those who feared the LORD', and then God speaks to 'you who revere my name' (3:16; 4:2).

Blaspheming the name of the Lord deserved the punishment of death by stoning (see Lev. 24:10–23). And the Lord Jesus told us to pray, 'Our Father in heaven, hallowed be your name' (Matt. 6:9). Despising the name of the Lord sounds like a precarious occupation, and in fact it is a serious sin.

In their response to this accusation, the priests reveal the immense gap between their perception of reality and God's perception, and also their instinctive tendency to doubt God and disagree with him (6–8).

Here is the practical daily evidence that the priests despise God. Sacrifices were meant to be of the highest quality, the best animals and the finest produce, appropriate for the God to whom they were offered. An animal sacrifice was to be without blemish or defect, and grain offerings were to be of the 'finest flour' (see Exod. 12:5; Lev. 1:3; 6:15). If the priests had read the Scriptures recently, they would have remembered these words from Leviticus:

> Do not bring anything with a defect, because it will not be accepted on your behalf . . . Do not offer to the LORD the blind, the injured or the maimed, or anything with warts or festering or running sores. Do not place any of these on the altar as a food offering presented to the LORD. (Lev. 22:20, 22)

---

[2] Wenham, *Leviticus*, p. 228.

Some of these sacrifices provided atonement for sin and forgiveness for sinners (see Lev. 1:1–17; 4:1 – 5:13). How bizarre to offer a sacrifice to cover sin, when the sacrifice itself was blind or lame! Other sacrifices were expressions of thanksgiving to God or dedication to God (see Lev. 2:1 – 3:17). How bizarre to offer a sacrifice that was meant to express dedication or thanksgiving, but was diseased! These blind, lame and diseased sacrifices revealed much about the worshippers who offered them, and even more about the priests who accepted them. It was not a matter of 'Only the best will do for God', but rather 'Give God the worst.' How typical of priests and people at that time that they did not have the nerve to actually stop offering sacrifices, but offered second-rate sacrifices, going through the motions of serving God when their hearts, lips and lives were far away from God.

Furthermore, the sacrifices that dealt with sin and brought atonement and forgiveness were meant to point forward to the sacrifice of Christ, just as the priests were meant to point forward to Christ our great high priest. As Calvin wrote of the priests, 'Since then they were in this respect the types of Christ, it behoved them to strive themselves to be holy . . . for the more excellent their condition was [i.e. priests], the more eminent ought to have been their piety and holiness.'[3]

To despise these sacrifices was to despise the heart of God's gospel provision for atonement, forgiveness and cleansing from sin, as we have seen. For we read in Hebrews that the earthly sanctuary pointed to Christ:

They serve at a sanctuary that is a copy and shadow of what is in heaven. This is why Moses was warned when he was about to build the tabernacle: 'See to it that you make everything according to the pattern shown you on the mountain' . . .

But when Christ came as high priest of the good things that are now already here, he went through the greater and more perfect tabernacle that is not made with human hands, that is to say, is not a part of this creation. He did not enter by means of the blood of goats and calves; but he entered the Most Holy Place once for all by his own blood, so obtaining eternal redemption.
(Heb. 8:5; 9:11–12)

---

[3] Calvin, on Mal. 1:9 in *Malachi*, p. 493.

As Malachi has already appealed to common values, so now he appeals to common decency, with the repeated question 'Is that not wrong?' *When you offer blind animals for sacrifice, is that not wrong? When you sacrifice lame or diseased animals, is that not wrong?* (8). He is using the motivation of common sense or common decency in a gracious attempt to help the priests and the people to recognize how awful is their behaviour. He continues with another appeal to common sense: *'Try offering them to your governor! Would he be pleased with you? Would he accept you?' says* the LORD *Almighty.*

We do not know if the priests led the way in this insult to God, or if the people led the way and the priests were too weak to put a stop to it. Either way they are responsible, because they are the ones who approve animals for sacrifices. They are responsible, because they are the religious leaders of God's community, of God's people. No wonder Malachi begs the priests to recognize their responsibility, their fault, their duty and their ministry, and to throw themselves on the grace of God: *Now plead with God to be gracious to us. With such offerings from your hands, will he accept you?* (9).

a. Calling all leaders

These words were not addressed to the people as a whole, as were the words in 1:2–5. This section is addressed to the *priests who show contempt for my name* (6). This is a double disgrace. For while there was a governor, who was responsible for civic welfare, it was the priests who were representatives of God the Lord of hosts, and it was their job to be examples of godly obedience, and to teach and train the people in godly obedience. It is a double disgrace because they were leaders of the community, and because they were God's representatives. If the leaders fail, no wonder the people are in trouble. If the leaders dishonour God whom they represent, no wonder the people are deep in shared corporate sin. If the leaders do not exercise discipline, there is little hope for the people.

The book of Malachi was a word from God which was designed to reform and transform the church of that day, the people of Israel. If you want to change a church, you must change the leaders. So Malachi addresses the priests in 1:6 – 2:9. Likewise today, if we want the word of God to reform and transform the church of God, we must address these words to the leaders of our churches. And we must preach them to ourselves, if we are leaders. Those who lead churches and influence their direction include ministers, preachers, the leadership committee, those who lead or teach in every area including youth and children's work, as well as those who mentor and train others, or lead or teach in home Bible studies. Such leaders set the standard for the church. They either rebuke or condone sin. They either model and encourage godliness or model and encourage ungodliness. They provide either a good example or a bad example.

And what is required of such leaders in these verses, and what challenge comes to us here? We need to have at the centre of our lives, at the centre of those we lead, at the centre of our church, a deep and growing awareness of the free and electing love of God. We need to see this love of God in terms of his rescue of us from damnation, his constant forgiveness and faithful mercy. For we also need to know that God is a holy God, pure and without sin, the judge of the whole world, who has called us to be his holy people. If we do not have this, we too will run the danger of despising God's name, God's character, God's revelation of himself. And the sign that we are doing this will be that we despise sacrifices. May our leaders lead us back to God!

b. Making use of this teaching

Old Testament sacrifices served three distinct purposes:

1. Atonement sacrifices, such as 'burnt offerings' and 'sin offerings', achieved forgiveness of sin and cleansing from sin (Lev. 1; 4:1 – 5:13). These were sacrifices offered by individuals, and also on behalf of the community, such as the daily morning and evening sacrifices, and the annual Day of Atonement sacrifices (Exod. 29:38–46; Lev. 16).
2. Other sacrifices, such as 'grain offerings' and 'fellowship' or 'peace' offerings, signified self-offering or consecration to God, thanksgiving to God, and fellowship with God (Lev. 2 – 3).
3. Sacrifices of animals, birds, oil, salt, flour and grain were also intended to teach God's people the need for self-sacrifice. Sacrifices should be offered by self-sacrificial people. This is shown in the strong condemnation of those who continued to offer sacrifices when their lives and hearts were far from obedience to God (Isa. 66:1–4; Amos 4:1–5).

How might we fall into the same trap of despising sacrifices?

i. Despising the sacrifice of Christ as the atonement for our sins

It is important to see Old Testament sacrifices as prefiguring the sacrifice of Christ. So in this case to despise the sacrifices is to despise Christ's great sacrifice made once for all 'for the sins of the whole world' (1 John 2:2).

We despise the sacrifice of Christ if we think that we don't need it, if we replace it with sacrifices that we make, if we think that it is an unacceptable idea in today's world, if we are embarrassed about it, or if we neglect to teach others about it in our evangelism. We despise the sacrifice of Christ if we think that we can approach God without claiming access to him solely through the blood of Christ. We despise the sacrifice of Christ if we do not constantly confess our sins and ask God to make us clean by the blood of Jesus. We despise the sacrifice of Christ if we continue in brazen sin. We despise the sacrifice of Christ if we think we can live without the protection of the blood of Christ from the power of Satan: 'They triumphed over him by the blood of the Lamb' (Rev. 12:11). We despise the sacrifice of Christ if we fail to preach 'Christ crucified' (1 Cor. 1:23). We despise the sacrifice of Christ if we turn away from his atoning death; if we join those who have 'trampled the Son of God underfoot, who [have] treated as an unholy thing the blood of the covenant that sanctified them, and who [have] insulted the Spirit of grace' (Heb. 10:29). And we despise this sacrifice if we fail to come into the Most Holy Place, the presence of God, with 'the full assurance that faith brings', by means of the blood of Jesus (see Heb. 10:19–22).

So we might neglect the great atoning sacrifice of Christ, fail to recognize that we are sinners who need an atoning sacrifice, fail to proclaim Christ crucified, and fail to see that we can enter into the presence of God only by means of the death of Christ.

ii. Despising our self-offering to God

We begin with Paul's great call to sacrifice in Romans:

> Therefore, I urge you, brothers and sisters, in view of God's mercy, to offer your bodies as a living sacrifice, holy and pleasing to God – this is your true and proper worship. Do not conform to the pattern of this world, but be transformed by the renewing of your mind. Then you will

be able to test and approve what God's will is – his good, pleasing and perfect will.
(Rom. 12:1–2)

In the following verses Paul develops that theme of offering living sacrifices as he talks about the corporate life of the people of God and how they relate to one another. It is not a call for individual sacrifice, but to a sacrificial pattern of using our gifts in the whole people of God.

The author of Hebrews writes of two sacrifices we should offer to God. The first is the praise of God in worship and evangelism, and the second is in doing good to others and sharing what we have.

Through Jesus, therefore, let us continually offer to God a sacrifice of praise – the fruit of lips that openly profess his name. And do not forget to do good and to share with others, for with such sacrifices God is pleased.
(Heb. 13:15–16)

Paul wrote of the sacrificial gifts of money sent by the Philippian church to support his ministry: 'I have received full payment and have more than enough. I am amply supplied, now that I have received from Epaphroditus the gifts you sent. They are a fragrant offering, an acceptable sacrifice, pleasing to God' (Phil. 4:18). And he also wrote of the self-sacrifice which comes from suffering persecution for doing gospel ministry:

But even if I am being poured out like a drink offering on the sacrifice and service coming from your faith, I am glad and rejoice with all of you. So you too should be glad and rejoice with me.
(Phil. 2:17–18)

Similarly Peter writes of spiritual sacrifices we should offer God, proclaiming his mighty acts in the world in our public witness and evangelism:

As you come to him, the living Stone – rejected by humans but chosen by God and precious to him – you also, like living stones, are being built into a spiritual house to be a holy priesthood, offering spiritual sacrifices acceptable to God through Jesus Christ . . . But you are a chosen people, a royal priesthood, a holy nation, God's special possession, that you may

declare the praises of him who called you out of darkness into his
wonderful light.
(1 Pet. 2:4–5, 9)

Despising these sacrifices might mean us failing to offer satisfactory
sacrifices of daily offering of ourselves to God, of the way we serve the
body of Christ, confess God's name and share what we have with those in
need, give money to support Christian ministry, or suffer for our public
presentation of the gospel (Rom. 12; Heb. 13; Phil. 2; 4).

iii. Despising our self-sacrificial lifestyle

The third way is to see that these sacrifices, fulfilled in Christ, point to the
life of self-sacrifice that we followers of Christ are called to embrace, in
imitation of Christ, by his grace. So we despise these sacrifices and the
sacrifice of Christ if we fail to 'accept one another … just as Christ
accepted you' or 'love one another' as God loved us when he sent his Son
as the Saviour of the world (Rom. 15:7; 1 John 4:7, 11). For 'this is how we
know what love is: Jesus Christ laid down his life for us. And we ought to
lay down our lives for our brothers and sisters' (1 John 3:16); and 'it has
been granted to you on behalf of Christ not only to believe in him, but also
to suffer for him' (Phil. 1:29).

So too Paul wrote of the need to forgive one another, following the
example of Christ's sacrifice:

Get rid of all bitterness, rage and anger, brawling and slander, along with
every form of malice. Be kind and compassionate to one another,
forgiving each other, just as in Christ God forgave you. Follow God's
example, therefore, as dearly loved children and live a life of love, just
as Christ loved us and gave himself up for us as a fragrant offering and
sacrifice to God.
(Eph. 4:31 – 5:2)

We might fail to live a life that reflects Christ's sacrifice by failing to
welcome one another, love one another, forgive one another, lay down our
lives for one another. Of course it is relatively easy to treat those we like
this way. We feel a natural affinity, they are less likely to offend us, and we
want to maintain our relationship with them, so we find it possible to
welcome, love, forgive and lay down our lives. But these instructions are

not about our close relationships; they are about how we treat all fellow believers. This is much more demanding, especially when they are wrong, thoughtless, offensive, rude, intolerant, sinful and sure they are right. And, to be honest, it is not always easy to offer the sacrifice of welcoming, loving, forgiving, and laying down our lives for those who are close to us! As someone put it, 'Who is our neighbour? Someone God puts near us to test our growth in Christ!'

c. A sacrificial church?

If we put together the different ideas of sacrifices in the New Testament, we can see how easily we might fall into the same trap as the people of God in Malachi's day, despising God's name by offering second-rate sacrifices – sacrifices that look good but are merely trivial, that have the appearance of godliness but not its substance, sacrifices that cost us nothing.

How can we know that we might run the danger of despising the sacrifice of Christ? It is because the people of God in Malachi's day despised their sacrifices, the very sacrifices that pointed forward to the sacrifice of Christ.

Offering a satisfactory sacrifice is more than simply being in favour of an idea. To offer a sacrifice is to live intentionally, to do what costs us dearly and to give up something, so that we can offer God the obedience and service that is his due. As King David said, 'I will not sacrifice to the LORD my God burnt offerings that cost me nothing' (2 Sam. 24:24). Yet the main point of sacrifices is not what they cost us, but whether they please God. We need a God-centred view of our sacrifices.

Is your church a sacrificial church? What does your church give up in order to offer it to God? Is your ministry a sacrificial ministry? What do you give up in order to do your ministry? Is your life a sacrificial life? What does it cost you to live as a Christian? Do you intentionally offer yourself each day to God as a living sacrifice? Do you offer each day as an occasion when you will give God gladly whatever he asks of you? Does your bank account speak of a sacrificial life? Is your social life sacrificial? Are your prayers sacrificial prayers, or are they self-centred and self-serving? What about your church's prayers: are they focused solely on the needs or wants of the church, or are they sacrificial prayers? And what about your church's use of its resources? Sacrificial or self-indulgent?

There are many arguments against sacrificial living. They surround us in our society, and infiltrate our thinking and our actions in our churches. Here are just a few:

Isn't self-sacrifice psychologically dangerous? Won't I damage my personality if I deny myself?

No, there is no danger in conscious and intentional self-denial and sacrifice. You will not warp yourself, as long as you intentionally deny yourself, having first counted the cost.

Isn't there a danger of obsessive self-sacrifice?

Yes, there is a danger, but don't feel that you have to go to that extreme, and don't let fear of extreme behaviour stop your basic Christian duty.

Surely Christ's great sacrifice means that we don't have to offer sacrifices; and isn't there a danger of thinking we are saving ourselves by our own sacrifices?

We are saved by Christ's sacrifice alone, but Christ who saved us by his sacrifice called us to follow him in the sacrifices that we make. As we are 'saved to serve', so we are 'saved to sacrifice'. It is not that we are saved by our sacrifices, but that they are a right response to God by people who have been saved.

If I don't have outstanding gifts, then there is no real value in my sacrifice.

No, God loves the loving sacrifices of all his children, and uses them for good.

Will self-sacrifice make me happy?

Perhaps that is not the best question to ask. We should be motivated by what God wants, not what we want. And in fact, if you can work through the pain, there can be joy in being set free from self-centredness. And ultimately God's glory will be our greatest joy.

Surely I need to establish myself in a good career and good income stream, and own my own home? Then I plan to make some sacrifices.

Well, you will only make it more difficult for yourself, because you will be accustomed to the higher lifestyle, and may find it almost impossible to change. A good guide is 'As now, so then'. That is, the kind of Christian life you live now shows you how you will live in the future.

Surely our church should build itself up first, and only then think of those outside, or Christians overseas.
Again, 'As now, so then' is a good guide to what will happen. A church which bases itself on selfishness will find it very difficult to change its ways.

Would it be all right to make sacrifices occasionally?
No, for the Lord Jesus told us to take up our cross daily in order to follow him, and Paul challenged us to offer ourselves as living sacrifices (Luke 9:23; Rom. 12:1–2).

Surely any sacrifice that we make is so unworthy that it insults God?
No, for the imperfections in our sacrifices are covered by the sacrifice of Christ: we are 'in Christ' and offer our sacrifices 'through Christ'. So God our heavenly Father will accept them for Christ's sake, and in Christ.

Forgive the dated language, but this haunting poem by the famous missionary to India Amy Carmichael is too good to miss.

Hast thou no scar?
No hidden scar on foot, or side, or hand?
I hear thee sung as mighty in the land;
I hear them hail thy bright, ascendant star.
Hast thou no scar?

Hast thou no wound?
Yet I was wounded by the archers; spent,
Leaned Me against a tree to die; and rent
By ravening beasts that compassed Me, I swooned.
Hast thou no wound?

No wound? No scar?
Yet, as the Master shall the servant be,
And piercèd are the feet that follow Me.
But thine are whole; can he have followed far
Who hast no wound or scar?[4]

---

[4] Amy Carmichael, 'No Scar?', <http://www.crossroad.to/Victory/poems/amy_carmichael/no-scar.htm>, accessed 17 May 2012.

2. Please shut the temple doors (1:10–14)

Malachi's temple was the second temple building in Jerusalem. The first was built by King Solomon (1 Kgs 6 – 8); later, when the Babylonians captured Jerusalem, this first temple was destroyed and many of the temple vessels were taken to Babylon. When the people of God came back from exile in Babylon they built the second temple, as we read in Ezra, prompted by the preaching of Haggai and Zechariah (Ezra 6:14).

We often think of the temple as symbolizing the presence of God among his people, as a kind of visual aid. It was more than that. It was the place where God made himself present on earth, and the ark of the covenant was his earthly throne in the temple as it had been in the tabernacle that was built under the leadership of Moses at Mount Sinai. That tent was a kind of movable temple, set up at Sinai, carried through the desert and set up whenever the people rested, and finally carried into the Promised Land and erected there. It preceded the first temple.

Here are the words that God used when he instructed Moses to build the tabernacle: 'Then let them make a sanctuary for me, and I will dwell among them' (Exod. 25:8). And when the tabernacle was completed, it was covered with the cloud, that visible sign of God's presence:

> Then the cloud covered the tent of meeting, and the glory of the LORD
> filled the tabernacle. Moses could not enter the tent of meeting because
> the cloud had settled on it, and the glory of the LORD filled the
> tabernacle.
> (Exod. 40:34–35)

The cloud by day and the fire by night was the sign of God's presence.

> Whenever the cloud lifted from above the tabernacle, they would set out;
> but if the cloud did not lift, they did not set out – until the day it lifted. So
> the cloud of the LORD was over the tabernacle by day, and fire was in the
> cloud by night, in the sight of all the Israelites during all their travels.
> (Exod. 40:36–38)

After they entered the Promised Land, they were instructed to set up one central sanctuary, which would be God's dwelling-place, where he would live among them. There they would meet in the presence of God.

But you are to seek the place the LORD your God will choose from among all your tribes to put his Name there for his dwelling. To that place you must go; there bring your burnt offerings and sacrifices, your tithes and special gifts . . . There, in the presence of the LORD your God, you and your families shall eat and shall rejoice.
(Deut. 12:5–7)

The central sanctuary became the temple. When Solomon dedicated the first temple he spoke of people praying towards it, and doing so because God's name was present in the temple.

Give attention to your servant's prayer and his plea for mercy, LORD my God. Hear the cry and the prayer that your servant is praying in your presence this day. May your eyes be open towards this temple night and day, this place of which you said, 'My Name shall be there', so that you will hear the prayer your servant prays towards this place. Hear the supplication of your servant and of your people Israel when they pray towards this place. Hear from heaven, your dwelling place, and when you hear, forgive.
(1 Kgs 8:28–30)

Of course God was not confined to the temple, but he made himself present there. No wonder the people prayed, 'You who sit enthroned between the cherubim, shine forth . . . Awaken your might; come and save us. Restore us, O God; make your face shine on us, that we may be saved' (Ps. 80:1–3). The point is that God's words *Oh, that one of you would shut the temple doors* (10) were not just a desire that people learn a lesson, but the desire that people would stay out of his presence on earth. God would prefer people to stay away, than come unwillingly, reluctantly, pretending worship and commitment that they did not intend. God's words here are reminiscent of his words through Isaiah many years before:

When you come to appear before me,
    who has asked this of you,
    this trampling of my courts?
Stop bringing meaningless offerings!
    Your incense is detestable to me . . .

When you spread out your hands in prayer,
    I hide my eyes from you;
even when you offer many prayers,
    I am not listening.
(Isa. 1:12–13, 15)

The temple is God's earthly home. He is asking his guests to leave. Here God says, through Malachi, that he does not enjoy their company, and so will not receive their offerings (10). They were misusing the very means that God had graciously put in place to make it possible for them to be in his presence, namely, the temple and the sacrifices. For temple worship and the offering of sacrifices were not human efforts to win God's favour, but gifts of God's grace, to enable his people to come before him with their sins forgiven, to express their thanksgiving, commitment and praise. The temple, the priests and the sacrifices were all provided by God; they were all his gracious gifts.

Furthermore, temple, priests and sacrifices were all visible signs of the Christ to come. God who made his name present in his glory in the temple would be personally present in his Son in his incarnate life. And this Son would fulfil the work of priests and sacrifices in his offering of himself once for all on the cross. If God's people despised temple and sacrifices, they would be unlikely to welcome the coming Messiah. This helps us see the deep significance of their actions and attitudes. Later Jesus himself cleansed the temple of its corruptions (John 2:13–22), as he also fulfilled its promise by his atoning death as priest and sacrifice (Heb. 9:1–14).

This section of Malachi also points to the frailty and sin of the priests. Ultimately the work of frail animals and frail, sinful and mortal priests will be finished when it is fulfilled and replaced in the work of Christ. As we read in Hebrews,

Now there have been many of those priests, since death prevented them from continuing in office; but because Jesus lives for ever, he has a permanent priesthood. Therefore he is able to save completely those who come to God through him, because he always lives to intercede for them.

Such a high priest truly meets our need – one who is holy, blameless, pure, set apart from sinners, exalted above the heavens. Unlike the other high priests, he does not need to offer sacrifices day after day, first for his own sins, and then for the sins of the people. He sacrificed for their sins once for all when he offered himself. For the law appoints as high priests men in all their weakness; but the oath, which came after the law, appointed the Son, who has been made perfect for ever. (Heb. 7:23–28)

Instead of these many sacrifices offered by many priests, Christ 'offered for all time one sacrifice for sins', and then he 'sat down at the right hand of God', his work of atonement completed (Heb. 10:12). So we are not being told to stay away from God because of defective and disobedient priests, but to draw near to God through Christ:

Therefore, brothers and sisters, since we have confidence to enter the Most Holy Place by the blood of Jesus, by a new and living way opened for us through the curtain, that is, his body, and since we have a great priest over the house of God, let us draw near to God with a sincere heart with the full assurance that faith brings, having our hearts sprinkled to cleanse us from a guilty conscience and having our bodies washed with pure water. Let us hold unswervingly to the hope we profess, for he who promised is faithful. And let us consider how we may spur one another on towards love and good deeds, not giving up meeting together, as some are in the habit of doing, but encouraging one another – and all the more as you see the Day approaching. (Heb. 10:19–25)

What a great antidote to the problems of Malachi's day!

a. My name is great among the nations (1:11)[5]

The point of this verse is clear, even if its full meaning is more difficult to find out. The point is the contrast between the attitude to God among the nations, and the attitude and actions of the priests of Malachi's day in verses 6–10 and 12–14. And the point of this verse is reinforced by the last section of verse 14, which shows the contrast between the priests' shoddy and shabby sacrifices in Jerusalem and the willing service and worship of God elsewhere throughout the world.

---

[5] Where the NIV uses the future tense in v. 11 (*My name will be great*), other translations have the present tense: 'My name *is* great among the nations.' Similarly in v. 14: 'my name *is* feared', where NIV has *My name is to be feared*.

However, the meaning of this willing worship of God elsewhere throughout the world is more difficult to discover. It is certainly universal throughout the world. It is *from where the sun rises to where it sets*. It is *in every place*; it is *among the nations*; and again it is *among the nations*.

Some take it to refer to the worship offered by Jews still in exile in Babylon, Assyria, Egypt and elsewhere. They were broadly scattered among the nations in Malachi's day, and could perhaps be described as being in every place from east to west. However, the verse seems to imply that the nations, the Gentiles, are those who offer this worship, and the message of the Old Testament seems to be that the godly remnant of God's people are those who have returned to Jerusalem.

Some take it to mean God-fearing Gentiles who joined in the worship of God's people, but there is no evidence that there were so many of these at that time, sufficient to justify the universal claim of the verse.

Some take it to refer to 'anonymous true believers' among all the nations, who may know nothing of God's Old Testament revelation, nothing of his words and works, his choice of Israel, of temple, priests, sacrifices or prophets, and yet who do worship the true God in the rituals of their own religions. This seems unlikely, because, as we have seen, the name of God means his self-revelation to Israel, his revealed character, and his presence in the temple. And there is no evidence elsewhere in the Old Testament that God would welcome pagan worship; in fact it is made clear that it is not acceptable (Exod. 32, as we have seen; 2 Kgs 22:3–17; Ezek. 8).

Or it could mean that the nations have learnt to respect the Lord, even if they do not serve him (see Ezek. 25:5–17; 26:6; 28:22; Dan. 3:28–29; Ezra 1:1–4; 6:9–12; 7:12–16). However, the verse indicates a more positive response to God than respect.

It would be unwise to adopt any of these views without more evidence and support from elsewhere in the Bible. It is always dangerous to adopt a view that is based on one verse, especially when these views are contradicted by clearer passages in the Bible. It is more likely that there is a future reference here, and certainly the words may be translated that way, as in the NIV translation.

If this is the case, then we are in familiar Bible territory, because it becomes a major theme of Old and New Testament alike – that of the conversion of the nations through the ministry of Jesus Christ's apostles.[6]

---

[6] Gen. 12:1–3; 1 Kgs 8:41–43; Pss 2; 110; 117; Isa. 42:1–9; 55; Jon.; Zech. 14; Matt. 28:16–20; Luke 24:45–49; Acts 2; 9:1–14; 10; 13 – 14; 28; Rom. 11; 15:7–13; Eph. 2:11 – 3:6; Rev. 5; 7; 21 – 22.

The Roman Catholic Church uses Malachi 1:11 as a prophecy of the offering of the Mass. If we meet this idea today, the best remedy is to emphasize that all the Old Testament sacrifices that dealt with sin were fulfilled in the sacrifice of Christ on the cross, and the action of the priests in offering those sacrifices was fulfilled in that same sacrifice. Old Testament sacrifices did achieve atonement, but their New Testament counterpart is not the Lord's Supper, but Christ's death on the cross. For that sacrifice was made once for all:

> But when Christ came . . . he entered the Most Holy Place once for all by
> his own blood, so obtaining eternal redemption.
> (Heb. 9:11–12)

> [Christ] has appeared once for all at the culmination of the ages to do
> away with sin by the sacrifice of himself.
> (Heb. 9:26)

> And by [God's] will, we have been made holy through the sacrifice of the
> body of Jesus Christ once for all.
> (Heb. 10:10)

And though Christ remains a priest for ever, he is not still offering his sacrifice in heaven:

> Day after day every priest stands and performs his religious duties; again
> and again he offers the same sacrifices, which can never take away sins.
> But when [Christ] had offered for all time one sacrifice for sins, he sat
> down at the right hand of God.
> (Heb. 10:11–12)

His sacrifice remains powerful for eternity, but he is not still offering it. Christ's atoning work is finished, so no earthly 'Mass' can be part of an eternal offering of Christ.

In summary, this verse contrasts the lack of willing obedience of the priests in Malachi's day with the future willing conversion of the nations. Jesus made a similar contrast:

> Many will come from the east and the west, and will take their places at
> the feast with Abraham, Isaac and Jacob in the kingdom of heaven. But

the subjects of the kingdom will be thrown outside, into the darkness,
where there will be weeping and gnashing of teeth.
(Matt. 8:11–12)

In the parable of the vineyard he warned God's people that 'the kingdom of
God will be taken away from you and given to a people who will produce its
fruit' (Matt. 21:43). And Paul's policy as the apostle to the nations was to
use their conversion to prompt the Jews to believe in the Messiah, Jesus:
'Inasmuch as I am the apostle to the Gentiles, I take pride in my ministry in
the hope that I may somehow arouse my own people to envy and save some
of them' (Rom. 11:13–14).

Indeed this use of the Gentiles to prod the Jews to respond to God was
foretold in Deuteronomy:

They made me jealous by what is no god,
  and angered me with their worthless idols.
I will make them envious by those who are not a people;
  I will make them angry by a nation that has no understanding.
(Deut. 32:21)

And the conversion of Gentiles is also a reminder to Israel that they too are
subjects of God's free mercy and grace, as we read in these words of the
prophet Hosea:

Yet the Israelites will be like the sand on the seashore, which cannot be
measured or counted. In the place where it was said to them, 'You are not
my people', they will be called, 'children of the living God'.
(Hos. 1:10)

So this interpretation fits in well with some major Bible themes, and
helps us understand a difficult verse. God will be praised, despite the sin
of his chosen people. God will raise up people to praise him, in whom his
transforming grace is effective and fruitful.

b. Profaning the Lord's name (1:12–13)

In contrast to this future worship of God is the attitude of God's people in
Malachi's day (12–13). These words seem to address both priests and
people. So the attitude of the leaders has infected the people, and the

leaders were unable to resist or question the actions of the people in bringing diseased animals for sacrifice. For the people chose the animals they would bring, and it was the job of the priests to accept the animal as suitable for sacrifice, or reject it.

To despise the name of the Lord (6) is to treat it as worthless; to *profane it* (12) is to treat it as unholy. The priests do this *by saying, 'The Lord's table is defiled,' and 'Its food is contemptible.'* Here we see that sins breed sins, and sins breed worse sins. They began by accepting worthless sacrifices; that then led to despising the table or altar on which the sacrifices were offered. The logic is that if the sacrifices are worthless, then the table must be worthless as well. So they despise the gracious gift of God, the means by which sin is atoned for and offerings are accepted. To despise God's gifts is to despise God; to treat God's gifts of grace as unholy is to reject the very means that God has provided for sins to be forgiven. And this attitude is then reflected in what they say, and so communicate to others, priests and worshippers alike: *'And you say, "What a burden!" and you sniff at it contemptuously,' says the* Lord *Almighty* (13). We see here a spiralling moral decline in which sin multiplies and intensifies.

c. Profanity today

The people and priests in Malachi's day were in a similar situation to some of God's people in New Testament times, reflected in the letter to the Hebrews, as we have seen. To despise God's means of atonement in any age is dangerous, and never more so than to turn away from Christ, God's great high priest and sacrifice. Apostasy from Christ leaves no place for forgiveness, because our forgiveness and cleansing is only in Christ.

> Anyone who rejected the law of Moses died without mercy on the testimony of two or three witnesses. How much more severely do you think someone deserves to be punished who has trampled the Son of God underfoot, who has treated as an unholy thing the blood of the covenant that sanctified them, and who has insulted the Spirit of grace? (Heb. 10:28–29)

How can those who spurn the Son of God, profane his blood and outrage the Spirit be forgiven? For they have repudiated the means of atonement, the means of forgiveness, the means of cleansing.

How else might we profane what is holy? Notice some more New Testament warnings about profanity:

1. Don't let bitterness spoil your shared holiness in the church by becoming profane like Esau:

> Make every effort to live in peace with everyone and to be holy; without holiness no one will see the Lord. See to it that no one falls short of the grace of God and that no bitter root grows up to cause trouble and defile many. See that no one is sexually immoral, or is godless [profane] like Esau, who for a single meal sold his inheritance rights as the oldest son.
> (Heb. 12:14–16)

2. Don't ignore the holiness of the church and despise it as if it is common or profane:

> Don't you know that you yourselves are God's temple and that God's Spirit lives among you? If anyone destroys God's temple, God will destroy that person; for God's temple is sacred, and you together are that temple.
> (1 Cor. 3:16–17)

> For whenever you eat this bread and drink this cup, you proclaim the Lord's death until he comes. So then, whoever eats the bread or drinks the cup of the Lord in an unworthy manner will be guilty of sinning against the body and blood of the Lord. Everyone ought to examine themselves before they eat of the bread and drink from the cup. For those who eat and drink without discerning the body of Christ eat and drink judgment on themselves.
> (1 Cor. 11:26–29)

3. Don't exchange the truth of the gospel of Christ for profane chatter and myths:

> If you point these things out to the brothers and sisters, you will be a good minister of Christ Jesus, nourished on the truths of the faith and of the good teaching that you have followed. Have nothing to do with godless myths and old wives' tales.
> (1 Tim. 4:6–7)

Timothy, guard what has been entrusted to your care. Turn away
from godless chatter and the opposing ideas of what is falsely called
knowledge, which some have professed and in so doing have
departed from the faith.
(1 Tim. 6:20–21)

Do your best to present yourself to God as one approved, a worker
who does not need to be ashamed and who correctly handles the
word of truth. Avoid godless chatter, because those who indulge in it
will become more and more ungodly. Their teaching will spread like
gangrene.
(2 Tim. 2:15–17)

4. Reject unchastity, and don't profane your bodies:

Flee from sexual immorality. All other sins a person commits are
outside the body, but whoever sins sexually, sins against their own body.
Do you not know that your bodies are temples of the Holy Spirit, who is
in you, whom you have received from God? You are not your own; you
were bought at a price. Therefore honour God with your bodies.
(1 Cor. 6:18–20)

d. Roadkill sacrifices (1:14)

Shoddy sacrifices, roadkill rituals, reveal what the priests think about the
need for atonement and about the significance of dedication, thanksgiving and fellowship with God. They demean God, and so, of course, they
demean themselves and their ministry. And their attitude is so powerful
it has spread to the people, resulting in rank hypocrisy. *Cursed is the cheat
who has an acceptable male in his flock and vows to give it, but then sacrifices a blemished animal to the Lord* (14). Why would people try this
deception? They would not succeed in fooling God. Would they succeed
in fooling their neighbours? Sin blinds, so in some way such cheats seem
to be fooling themselves. One of the consequences of telling lies is that we
end up not trusting others, so one of the consequences of deceiving others
is that we only succeed in deceiving ourselves. This hypocrisy brings
about the covenant curse of God, because it adds attempted deception to
stinginess, the failure to give God what is his due: *Cursed is the cheat.*

And all this is so futile, *'For I am a great king,'* says the LORD Almighty,
'and my name is to be feared among the nations.' They will not get away

61

with their shoddy sacrifices, with despising God's name, with treating the table in the temple as polluted, with offering roadkill, with attempting to trick God, because God, *the* LORD *Almighty*, is *a great king*. And even if they are slow to praise and sloppy in their worship, God is still *the* LORD *Almighty*, truly worshipped and served by all the angels, and will be *feared among the nations*. So the priests and people of Malachi's day needed to learn again a great truth: God's love is a free gift that cannot be earned, and God's love demands total obedience. For, as they could read in Deuteronomy, 'the LORD . . . set his affection on you and [chose] you . . . because the LORD loved you'; and 'Love the LORD your God with all your heart and with all your soul and with all your strength' (Deut. 7:7–8; 6:5). God's love is a free gift that costs everything to receive.

e. Self-deception today

We of course are utterly amazed at the self-deception that abounded in Malachi's day. How could priests and people think that such actions would be satisfactory? How could there be such a gap between what God said and what they thought and said and did? Of course it is always easier to see sin in someone else than it is to see it in yourself.

Here is a trivial example. I frequently ride my bicycle around inner-city Melbourne. Occasionally, for the sake of convenience, I ride on the pedestrian pavement, especially at the beginning or the end of my journey. When I do so, I know that the pedestrians are perfectly safe, because I am such an expert cyclist that I can easily avoid any danger to them. Why should they worry? However, when I am a pedestrian, the situation is completely different. If someone else is riding a bicycle on the pavement where I am walking, I regard this as behaviour that is reckless, dangerous, selfish, self-indulgent, stupid and a threat to public safety. How my attitude changes! And how inconsistent I am!

When we look at the people of God in Malachi's day, it is like looking in a mirror. We see ourselves. And what we see is how easily the people of God are blinded to reality, how easily sin blinds them, and so how easily sin blinds us. All through the book of Malachi, there is this very disturbing gap between what God sees and what the people see, between what God says and what the people say. We have seen some examples here in chapter 1: '"I have loved you," says the LORD. 'But you ask, "How have you loved us?"' (1:2).

The reality is that we are most aware of the faults and sins of others, and most blind to our own faults and sins. And we are easily seduced by fiction away from fact. We are easy targets for imagining that our lives are satisfactory, when in reality they are not.

Our trouble is that we naturally think that we see things clearly, and we do not. And our Western world is especially vulnerable to fiction, because it is such a common drug. Daniel Boorstin produced his book *The Image: A Guide to Pseudo-events in America* in 1962. He wrote,

> We risk being the first people in history to have been able to make their illusions so vivid, so persuasive, so 'realistic' that they can live in them. We are the most illusioned people on earth. We dare not become disillusioned, because our illusions are the very house in which we live; they are our news, our heroes, our adventure, our forms of art, our very experience.[7]

He quotes Max Frisch's comment 'Technology . . . the knack of so arranging the world that we don't have to experience it', and gives the example of the following dialogue:

> Admiring friend: 'My, that's a beautiful baby you have there!'
> Mother: 'Oh, that's nothing. You should see his photograph!'[8]

Boorstin notes that 'news making' has replaced 'news gathering'; that celebrities have replaced real heroes; that tourists have replaced travellers; and that fiction is the greatest reality. For these pseudo-events are more dramatic, more vivid, more expensive, more intelligible, and more sociable.[9] It is remarkable to read these words written in the early 1960s. Images have become even more powerful and even more pervasive today: there is no undoctored reality in our daily lives. Boorstin did not write from a Christian perspective, but we can hear his call to reality and apply it to our receiving God's words in Scripture:

> We should try to reach beyond our images. We should seek new ways of letting messages reach us: from our own past, from God, from the world

---

[7] D. Boorstin, *The Image: A Guide to Pseudo-events in America* (New York: Harper & Row, 1962), p. 240.

[8] Ibid., pp. i, 7.

[9] Ibid., pp. 39, 40.

which we may hate or think we hate. To give visas to strange and alien and outside notions.[10]

John Calvin uses the wonderful image of the Scriptures as a pair of spectacles, or glasses, which enable us to see clearly. 'For just as eyes, when dimmed with age or weakness or by some other defect, unless aided by spectacles, discern nothing distinctly; so, such is our feebleness, unless Scripture guides us in seeking God, we are immediately confused.'[11] This is what was happening through Malachi's prophecy. The people did not see reality: God's words through Malachi were like spectacles to enable them to see clearly. So too these words of Scripture can do the same for us.

Of course, unreality is not confined to Western society. Lawrence of Arabia met a different kind of unreality in his colleagues Zeki and Nesib, as they rode through the desert on their camels:

When he pointed out that Zeki's camel was full of mange, Zeki launched into a long discourse on the 'Veterinary Department of State', minutely organised and scientifically equipped that would be established . . . [sometime in the future]. He and Nesib became so absorbed in planning its organisation during the next few days that they ignored all reminders about dressing the camel's itching skin – until, at last, it died.[12]

In fact, blindness to reality is universal, unless God opens our eyes, for as Paul wrote:

The god of this age has blinded the minds of unbelievers, so that they cannot see the light of the gospel that displays the glory of Christ, who is the image of God. For what we preach is not ourselves, but Jesus Christ as Lord, and ourselves as your servants for Jesus' sake. For God, who said, 'Let light shine out of darkness,' made his light shine in our hearts to give us the light of the knowledge of God's glory displayed in the face of Jesus Christ.
(2 Cor. 4:4–6)

---

[10] Ibid., pp. 260, 261.

[11] Calvin, *Institutes*, 1.14.1.

[12] B. H. L. Hart, *Lawrence of Arabia* (Cambridge: Da Capo Press, 1989 [1937]) p. 148.

As Iris Murdoch once commented: 'We live in a fantasy world, a world of illusion. The great task in life is to find reality.'[13] To do this we need the compassion of God, the transforming power of Christ, and the Spirit-inspired Holy Scriptures.

---

[13] *The Times*, 15 April 1983, 'Profile'.

Malachi 2:1–9

4. Honour my name

In this section, Malachi continues to address the priests. Twice he warns them of judgment (verses 1–3 and 8–9), and in verses 4–7 he reminds them of the good model of priesthood found in their ancestor Levi. The high calling they have as priests in Levi's line brings great responsibility. For great blessing leads to great responsibility, which brings the danger of great judgment.

1. The priests' responsibility

In 1:6–14, the issue being addressed was that of the sacrifices the priests accepted and offered to God; here in 2:1–9, it is the other responsibility of the priests that is in mind, that of teaching the law to the people, and setting them a good example. We often think of Old Testament priests as solely concerned with offering sacrifices, but they were also to keep, read, teach and apply the law of Moses to the people. So we read of Moses blessing the tribe of priests in these words: 'He watched over your word and guarded your covenant. He teaches your precepts to Jacob and your law to Israel' (Deut. 33:9–10; see also Jer. 18:18). In Haggai we find these words which refer to this ministry: 'Ask the priests what the law says' (Hag. 2:11). Chronicles refers to a time when the knowledge of God was missing from the life of the people: 'For a long time Israel was without the true God, without a priest to teach and without the law' (2 Chr. 15:3). And it seems as if this was also the situation in Malachi's day: *For the lips of a priest ought to preserve knowledge, because he is the messenger of the LORD Almighty and people seek instruction from his mouth* (7).

Indeed it looks as if a long-term problem is repeating itself, for if the priests had done their job and taught and applied the law of Moses, there would not have been such a great need for prophets to recall the people to obedience. However, in Malachi's day, it seems that the priests have been neglecting both aspects of their ministry: sacrifices and teaching. Of course it makes some kind of grim sense. If they do not honour God by offering right sacrifices, then they will not honour God by teaching his law.

As they disgrace God, so he threatens to disgrace them, and make their valuable ministry worthless (1–3). We may recoil from these harsh words, but warning people of the danger that they are in is a kindness, an act of grace: *If you do not listen* (2). God has told them that they 'show contempt for my name' (1:6), so now he summons them to a deep repentance, to *resolve to honour my name.* The best antidote to sin is righteousness, the best antidote to hatred is love, and the best antidote to despising God's revealed character and presence is to decide, to *resolve,* to *honour* God's *name.*

As they have corrupted their ministry of offering sacrifices, so God warns that he will pronounce the covenant curse, and put it into practice by cursing their blessings: *I will send a curse on you, and I will curse your blessings* (2). Indeed he has already done this, and corrupted their ministry of blessing the people: *I will curse your blessings. Yes, I have already cursed them, because you have not resolved to honour me.* They are meant to receive and share the blessings of the covenant, but they will both suffer and spread God's curses if they do not repent and *resolve to honour* God and his name. God will curse them by rendering them ceremonially unclean and so unfit to serve: *I will rebuke your descendants; I will smear on your faces the dung from your festival sacrifices* (3). And so they will be carried away with the refuse, out of the temple: *and you will be carried off with it.*

When the contemporary examples of priesthood were so appalling, the Lord through Malachi provided a moving picture of godly priesthood, to rebuke the priests and also to invite them to repentance, and show them how they should act (4–7). Levi was the ancestor of the priests and Levites of the people of God. The tribe of Levi showed its commitment to the Lord when Israel made a golden calf at Mount Sinai and worshipped it. Moses summoned the tribe of Levi to act in judgment. The sons of Levi did as Moses commanded, and about three thousand of the people were killed on that day. Moses said, 'You have been set apart to the LORD today, for you were against your own sons and brothers, and he has blessed you this day' (see Exod. 32:25–29).

Similarly Phinehas, another of the priestly tribe of Levi, acted decisively when the Moabites tried to seduce Israel. The Lord commended Phinehas, and in doing so referred to 'the covenant of peace' also found in Malachi 2:5.

> The LORD said to Moses, 'Phinehas son of Eleazar, the son of Aaron, the priest, has turned my anger away from the Israelites. Since he was as zealous for my honour among them as I am, I did not put an end to them in my zeal. Therefore tell him I am making my covenant of peace with him. He and his descendants will have a covenant of a lasting priesthood, because he was zealous for the honour of his God and made atonement for the Israelites.'
> (See Num. 25:1–13)

This example of Phinehas was celebrated in the Psalms:

> They yoked themselves to the Baal of Peor
>   and ate sacrifices offered to lifeless gods;
> they aroused the LORD's anger by their wicked deeds,
>   and a plague broke out among them.
> But Phinehas stood up and intervened,
>   and the plague was checked.
> This was credited to him as righteousness
>   for endless generations to come.
> (Ps. 106:28–31)

So Levi and his tribe had a high calling as priests of the Lord, and some, notably Phinehas, had honoured God in their actions.

Malachi drew attention to the attitude that should lie at the heart of priesthood, as of all servants of the Lord, namely reverence for the name of the Lord, for his personal revelation and his presence in the temple: *this called for reverence and he revered me and stood in awe of my name* (5). Those who revere God and God's name will teach God's people the truth, and will not teach error: *True instruction was in his mouth and nothing false was found on his lips* (6). This reverence for God and his revelation leads to integrity, and integrity leads to effective ministry: *He walked with me in peace and uprightness, and turned many from sin.* For the priests, as teachers of the law of Moses, were messengers of the Lord (as the prophet Malachi is as well): *For the lips of a priest ought to preserve knowledge, because he is the messenger of the LORD Almighty and people seek instruction from his mouth* (7). If only the priests had lived up to this standard, then the people might well have loved and served God with a whole heart.

However, the priests had done exactly the opposite, and instead had wreaked havoc. They had turned away from God, and so caused confusion among the people: *But you have turned from the way and by your teaching have caused many to stumble* (8). They had damaged themselves, and damaged others. They had betrayed their calling and broken their ancestral covenant, and so God declares he will disgrace them before the people:

> *'You have violated the covenant with Levi,' says the LORD Almighty.*
> *'So I have caused you to be despised and humiliated before all the people,*
> *because you have not followed my ways but have shown partiality in*
> *matters of the law.'*
> (8–9)

The priest had failed to follow the instruction written in Leviticus: 'Keep my commands and follow them. I am the LORD. Do not profane my holy name, for I must be acknowledged as holy by the Israelites. I am the LORD, who made you holy' (Lev. 22:31–32). No wonder God later provided Jesus, our great high priest, who was 'holy, blameless, pure, set apart from sinners, exalted above the heavens' (Heb. 7:26), for although he was the Son of God, 'he learned obedience from what he suffered and, once made perfect, he became the source of eternal salvation for all who obey him' (Heb. 5:8–9), with the result that 'we have been made holy through the sacrifice of the body of Jesus Christ once for all' (Heb. 10:10).

2. Church leaders today

Of course God's people today do not have nor need Old Testament priests to offer sacrifices, because that ministry was fulfilled in Christ.[1] But God

---

[1] I know that many Anglican churches still use the title 'priest'. But it is clear from the Book of Common Prayer that the Lord's Supper is not a sacrifice to take away sins. The title 'priest' must be understood as minister or elder.

does provide leaders for his people, and churches without leaders are incomplete. And, as in Malachi's day, good leaders bring great blessing and bad leaders cause chaos. Paul lists two requirements of church leaders in his letter to Titus: that they set a good example of life and godliness, and that they are able to teach truth and correct error.

> The reason I left you in Crete was that you might put in order what was left unfinished and appoint elders in every town, as I directed you. An elder must be blameless, faithful to his wife, a man whose children believe and are not open to the charge of being wild and disobedient. Since an overseer manages God's household, he must be blameless – not overbearing, not quick-tempered, not given to drunkenness, not violent, not pursuing dishonest gain. Rather, he must be hospitable, one who loves what is good, who is self-controlled, upright, holy and disciplined. He must hold firmly to the trustworthy message as it has been taught, so that he can encourage others by sound doctrine and refute those who oppose it.
> (Titus 1:5–9)

These qualities are reminiscent of Malachi 2:1–9, as is the warning in James: 'Not many of you should become teachers, my fellow believers, because you know that we who teach will be judged more strictly' (Jas 3:1).

May God raise up such leaders for his church today in every land, and continue to raise up such leaders for future generations.

Malachi 2:10–16

5. Do not be unfaithful

This section of Malachi does not primarily focus on the way the people were treating their God, but rather on the way in which they were treating one another. They were being 'unfaithful' to one another. Unfaithfulness is the main theme of this passage; the word 'unfaithful' appears five times in 2:10–16. Why then are we *unfaithful to one another?* (10) is the searching question that begins the passage. However, this section also makes it clear that being unfaithful to others entails being unfaithful to God. For the unity of God's people came from the fact that they had *one Father*, and *one God* (10).

Why does being unfaithful matter? Why does being faithful matter? The ultimate answer lies in who God is. The Lord God is the patron saint of faithfulness! The great claim of the Bible is that God is faithful in character, unchanging in his power, his love, his holiness, his grace and his gospel purposes.[1] And not only is God faithful in character in himself, he is also faithful to his words and his promises to us (see Pss 89:1–8, 14, 28, 33–37; 119:86, 138). This represents God's great commitment to us: that he makes verbal promises openly and publicly, and then keeps his promises. He makes himself publicly accountable for his faithful character by making himself publicly accountable in keeping his word. The formal promises of God are his covenants, his spoken and written promises (see Gen. 8:21–22; 9:9–17; 12:1–3; 17:1–14; Exod. 20 – 24). Covenants are a major theme in Malachi (see 2:4–5, 8, 10, 14; 3:1).

God is faithful to his people, and calls his people to be faithful to him. In Deuteronomy we find these same themes of the faithfulness of God the

---

[1] See Exod. 34:6–7; Pss 17:7; 25:6; 36:10; 48:9; 63:3; 107:43; Isa. 54:8, 10; Jer. 31:3; Joel 2:13; Neh. 9:17.

rock, the father and creator of his people, and the unfaithfulness of his people.

> He is the Rock, his works are perfect,
>   and all his ways are just.
> A faithful God who does no wrong,
>   upright and just is he.

> They are corrupt and not his children;
>   to their shame they are a warped and crooked generation.
> Is this the way you repay the LORD,
>   you foolish and unwise people?
> Is he not your Father, your Creator,
>   who made you and formed you?
> (Deut. 32:4–6)

When God's people turn away from God they are unfaithful, especially when they turn to other gods in idolatry:

> You deserted the Rock, who fathered you;
>   you forgot the God who gave you birth.

> The LORD saw this and rejected them
>   because he was angered by his sons and daughters . . .
> for they are a perverse generation,
>   children who are unfaithful.
> (Deut. 32:18–20)

God's people are called not only to be faithful to God, but also faithful to one another, within the covenant community of God's people, as we see here in Malachi. God who is faithful to his promises to his people calls his people to be faithful to him. God loves faithful people, so of Hanani, colleague of Nehemiah, we read, 'he was a faithful man and feared God more than many' (Neh. 7:2, NRSV).

Psalm 15 celebrates and calls for this kind of faithfulness:

> LORD, who may dwell in your sacred tent?
>   Who may live on your holy mountain?

The one whose way of life is blameless,
  who does what is righteous,
  who speaks the truth from their heart;
whose tongue utters no slander,
  who does no wrong to a neighbour,
  and casts no slur on others . . .
who keeps an oath even when it hurts.
(Ps. 15:1–4)

Faithfulness or trustworthiness is a great virtue: God's people are to keep their word. It is a tragedy when people are unreliable, untrustworthy and unfaithful to one another: 'Many claim to have unfailing love, but a faithful person who can find?' (Prov. 20:6). So, in Malachi, the faithful God calls his people to be faithful to him, and to be faithful to one another.

The call to be faithful to one another in this passage is based on the unity God's people have in God himself: *Do we not all have one Father? Did not one God create us? Why do we profane the covenant of our ancestors by being unfaithful to one another?* (10). Family loyalty should bind them to one another, for they have *one Father*, who has 'created' them to be his people. Their disloyalty to one another breaks their relationship not only with God but also with their *ancestors*.

This call to family loyalty is more than the kind of family loyalty which is found in most societies. For God's people are a special family, who have a special relationship with God who has made them his people, and also a special relationship with their ancestors, because they are descendants of Abraham, each one of them part of one of the twelve tribes of Israel. As God is their *one Father*, because he called them into being, and made them his special people, so they are also physically descended from the same *ancestors*.

It is very important that we pay close attention to the evidence that the people have been unfaithful. What were their sins? There were five of them. We need to distinguish them, to fully understand what was happening:

1. They have *desecrated the sanctuary the LORD loves* (11–12).
2. They have done this by *marrying women who worship a foreign god*: women from outside Israel who still remained idolaters (11).
3. They have divorced their Israelite wives in order to marry foreign wives (13–15).

73

4. Their marriage to idolaters will result in a failure to produce *godly offspring* (15).
5. They have engaged in *violence* (16).

We will look at each of these in more detail, but notice how their sins accumulated. Their central sin is that of marrying idolaters; the other sins link to this sin, whether as a way of doing it, or as a consequence of doing it. It is instructive to notice how inevitably a sin forms a cluster of other sins that are consequences of the central sin, or accompany that sin, or are committed to cover up the central sin.

Let's look at these sins in order.

1. Desecrating the sanctuary of the Lord (2:11–12)

God is a holy God. God has made his people holy and God calls his people to be holy. So desecrating what God has made holy is a significant and serious sin. To desecrate is to treat as common, to ignore or profane holiness. To desecrate what God has made holy is to desecrate God's holiness.

What is this *sanctuary*, or holy place? It could mean the holy temple, the holy sanctuary, where the holy God lives among his people. This is the most frequent meaning of the word 'sanctuary': 'let them make a sanctuary for me, and I will dwell among them' (Exod. 25:8). This is supported by the references to *the Lord's altar* in 2:13. Alternatively, *the sanctuary the Lord loves* could mean the holy people of God, for they are 'a holy nation', 'my treasured possession', 'the holy seed' (Exod. 19:6, 5; Isa. 6:13; Ezra 9:2). And they are called to be holy: 'You are to be holy to me because I, the Lord, am holy, and I have set you apart from the nations to be my own' (Lev. 20:26). This is supported by the reference to *godly* or 'holy' *offspring* in 2:15, since the production of holy offspring is endangered by marriage to idolaters.

These two meanings are really fairly close together, because in either case the people are desecrating what God has made holy. They are either desecrating the temple, God's sanctuary, or they are desecrating themselves, God's holy nation. I think that in the context the word 'sanctuary' is more likely to mean the temple, as idolatry directly endangers the holiness of the temple. It had happened before, as in the time of Athaliah, Manasseh and Zedekiah (see e.g. 2 Chr. 24:7; 33:3–4; Ezek. 8).

Though the central sin is that of marrying foreign idolaters, in desecrating what is holy they were desecrating the holy God who lived among them in his holy temple, and who had made them to be his holy people. We have already seen some New Testament warnings against desecrating or profaning holiness. These include turning away from Christ's atoning death; following Esau's example in failing to obtain the grace of God and pursue holiness; desecrating the church, the temple of the Holy Spirit, by destroying it; profaning the truth by exchanging it for profane chatter; or desecrating our bodies, temples of the Holy Spirit, by engaging in sexual immorality (Heb. 10:29; 12:16; 1 Cor. 3:17; 6:18–20; 1 Tim. 6:20).

One of the saddest features of human nature is that when we find something wonderful, we are tempted to bring it down to our level. We inscribe our names on precious buildings or special places; we want to read about the trashy side of famous people; and we want to simplify matters that are rightly demanding. We do these things to our loss. We do the same to God to our peril.

2. Marrying foreign women (2:11)

The condemnation of intermarriage is worth discussing because it seems alien and remote to us. We find it hard to understand, because we rightly attempt to refrain from racism, we enjoy food and people from many cultures (notice the order!), and we value our freedom to make our own choices about who we marry. When the Bible seems alien to us, we have to work hard to break through the barriers to make sense of it, and to understand its relevance to us.

a. Not racism but holiness

The first thing to say is that what we have here is not racism. The point was not the race of the women, it was that they were those *who worship a foreign god*. We see in Ezra 6 that God's people welcomed converted Gentiles to join them in the Passover: 'So the Israelites who had returned from the exile ate it, together with all who had separated themselves from the unclean practices of their Gentile neighbours in order to seek the LORD, the God of Israel' (Ezra 6:21). This had been legitimate since the Passover was instituted. Ruth, for example, was from Moab, but she had abandoned the Moabite gods, and taken on the service of the God of Israel (see Exod. 12; Ruth 1:16).

The second is that the division between Jews and Gentiles has been taken away by the death of Christ in the New Testament:

> Therefore, remember that formerly you who are Gentiles by birth and called 'uncircumcised' by those who call themselves 'the circumcision' (which is done in the body by human hands) – remember that at that time you were separate from Christ, excluded from citizenship in Israel and foreigners to the covenants of the promise, without hope and without God in the world. But now in Christ Jesus you who once were far away have been brought near by the blood of Christ.
>
> For he himself is our peace, who has made the two groups one and has destroyed the barrier, the dividing wall of hostility, by setting aside in his flesh the law with its commands and regulations. His purpose was to create in himself one new humanity out of the two, thus making peace, and in one body to reconcile both of them to God through the cross, by which he put to death their hostility. He came and preached peace to you who were far away and peace to those who were near.
> (Eph. 2:11–17)

So believers in Christ should not support racism. All human beings are of one blood (Acts 17:26), and are all equally made in the image of God (Gen. 1:26–27). The division instituted by God between his chosen people, the descendants of Abraham, and the other nations has now been erased by the death of Christ. We must repudiate racism.

But, if it is not racism, what is this condemnation of marrying these foreign women? The answer is that God is holy. God has made his people holy. God wants his people to be holy (Lev. 11:45). To be holy means to be wholly devoted to God, to share God's values, to obey God's will, to trust God's promises, to keep God's covenant, to live to God's glory. To be holy is not to be neutral; it is to be transformed by God, and to be committed to God. Foreigners could be included in the nation without polluting it, as long as men were circumcised, and as long as they turned away from idolatry, kept the law and the covenant, and worshipped and served the true and living God.

God's people were thrown out of the land because of their idolatry, so it was especially foolish of them to head in that same direction again. Solomon had previously led them into idolatry by marrying foreign wives (1 Kgs 11:1–13). As Joyce Baldwin comments, 'Since apostasy had been responsible for the exile, it was unthinkable that the whole community should be put at risk again.'[2]

So the point is not racism, but the requirement that the people of Israel follow the first two of the Ten Commandments:

> I am the Lord your God, who brought you out of Egypt, out of the land of slavery.
> You shall have no other gods before me.
> You shall not make for yourself an image in the form of anything in heaven above or on the earth beneath or in the waters below. You shall not bow down to them or worship them.
> (Exod. 20:2–5)

b. What about us?

The first point to make is that for New Testament believers in Christ there are no prohibitions on marrying someone of another race, ethnicity, tribe, culture or social group. While there is still deep racism in many people, we must not be controlled by that sinful attitude. Our unity in the human race is stronger than our divisions, and we are indeed all one in Christ Jesus. 'Here there is no Gentile or Jew, circumcised or uncircumcised, barbarian, Scythian, slave or free, but Christ is all, and is in all' (Col. 3:11).

The second point to make is that we are wise to marry a fellow believer in Christ. So Paul encouraged a wife who is considering remarriage after the death of her husband that 'she is free to marry anyone she wishes, only in the Lord' (1 Cor. 7:39, NRSV).

Does the New Testament forbid a believer to marry an unbeliever? It would seem so from 2 Corinthians: 'Do not be yoked together with unbelievers' (2 Cor. 6:14). However, there is no suggestion in the context of 2 Corinthians 6 that Paul was writing about marriage. The point he made was about joining with idolaters, as we see from the surrounding verses.

So this is not primarily about marriage, nor is it about leaving a corrupt church (see 2 Cor. 6:14–18),[3] but it does apply to entering into a marriage which would involve engaging in idolatry. Paul was warning the believers

---

[2] Baldwin, *Haggai, Zechariah, Malachi*, p. 238.
[3] The Old Testament references quoted are about leaving Babylon. Barnett, *Second Epistle to the Corinthians*, p. 344.

not to take part in pagan idolatrous worship, which was such a natural and common activity in Corinth at the time. As he wrote in 1 Corinthians:

> The sacrifices of pagans are offered to demons, not to God, and I do not want you to be participants with demons. You cannot drink the cup of the Lord and the cup of demons too; you cannot have a part in both the Lord's table and the table of demons. Are we trying to arouse the Lord's jealousy? Are we stronger than he?
> (1 Cor. 10:20–22)

This does not mean that the believers in Corinth should have no contact with unbelievers, as Paul also makes clear in 1 Corinthians.

> I wrote to you in my letter not to associate with sexually immoral people – not at all meaning the people of this world who are immoral, or the greedy and swindlers, or idolaters. In that case you would have to leave this world.
> (1 Cor. 5:9–10)

He will even allow believers to eat meat from the market, even though it might have been offered to an idol beforehand (1 Cor. 10:23–30). But it does mean that while in full contact with the world, we must guard against formal associations that would corrupt us. We are called to be 'in the world', but not 'of the world'. Indeed, we are sent 'into the world'. As Jesus prayed for his disciples:

> My prayer is not that you take them out of the world but that you protect them from the evil one. They are not of the world, even as I am not of it. Sanctify them by the truth; your word is truth. As you sent me into the world, I have sent them into the world.
> (John 17:15–18)

Furthermore, we also see that if a believer is already married to an unbeliever, Paul does not require divorce: on the contrary, he encourages the believer to stay married in order to win that person to Christ.

> To the rest I say this (I, not the Lord): If any brother has a wife who is not a believer and she is willing to live with him, he must not divorce her. And

if a woman has a husband who is not a believer and he is willing to live with her, she must not divorce him . . . But if the unbeliever leaves, let it be so. The brother or the sister is not bound in such circumstances; God has called us to live in peace. How do you know, wife, whether you will save your husband? Or, how do you know, husband, whether you will save your wife?
(1 Cor. 7:12–13, 15–16)

In many societies in the world, a Christian may have little choice about who he or she marries, because such decisions are made by parents or families. In those cases, a Christian may be 'unequally yoked' with an unbeliever by the decision of others. In that situation, this instruction from Paul would apply.

We should also note that while Malachi warned the Israelites not to divorce their wives and marry idolaters, he did not give any instruction to those who had done so. Should they then divorce their pagan spouses, and remarry their former partners? Malachi does not answer that question. However, in Ezra 9 and 10, we read of Israelites who had married idolaters (there is no suggestion that they had been already married within Israel). There Ezra required them to send away their foreign wives. This would mean that those women would return to their parents' families.

Whatever happened in the days of Malachi or Ezra, our situation as Christian believers is different, and we should follow Paul's instructions as outlined above.

3. Divorcing their Israelite wives (2:13–15)

The situation was further complicated and the sin compounded because in order to marry foreign wives, the Israelite men had divorced their Israelite wives (14–15).

a. God loves marriage

Notice the beautiful description of marriage in these verses: *the wife of your youth, your partner* and *the wife of your marriage covenant.* They were long-term marriages: marriage was all about companionship and partnership, and marriage was made by covenant, that is, by promise. This is a very high view of marriage, and in fact the most positive statement about marriage in the Old Testament, because the important word 'covenant' is only occasionally used of marriage. God made and designed marriage, and according to Genesis, marriage provides a helping partnership, and makes man and wife 'one flesh' (Gen. 2:18–24).[4]

God loves marriage, and gave us marriage as a good gift. Good marriages bring great blessing to husband and wife, to any children who are born of the marriage, to the extended family, to the local community and to society as a whole. Of course we humans have infinite creativity and energy to corrupt all of God's good gifts, not least marriage. The closeness of marriage can become a prison, married people can engage in physical or psychological abuse, people can be bad parents, and married couples can either selfishly idolize their marriages or despise their marriages and their partner. However, God loves marriage; it is a good gift to be received with praise and thanksgiving, and it should be cherished and nurtured.

Because God loves marriage, 'I hate divorce' (16, NRSV). The text does not say that God hates divorced people. It is because God knows the good power of marriage that he hates its destruction. And God certainly does not hate those Israelite women who have been so wantonly discarded by their husbands. It is because God wanted to protect women from being treated that way that he declared 'I hate divorce.' And God stands watch over their marriages: *the LORD is the witness between you and the wife of your youth. You have been unfaithful to her* (14). The covenant Lord is the witness to the covenant of marriage: and he defends marriages by speaking against those who would destroy them.

The purpose of this emphatic statement from God is to stop any Israelite man who is thinking of divorcing his wife to marry a woman from outside Israel.

When God tells us what he hates, it is in order to warn us away from such behaviour. So God hates temple worship when the people who offer it are unrepentant murderers and oppressing others: 'Your New Moon feasts and your appointed festivals I hate with all my being' (Isa. 1:14). Similarly, because God loves justice, he hates injustice: 'For I, the LORD, love justice; I hate robbery and wrongdoing' (Isa. 61:8). So too God hates the planning of evil, and lies, deceptions and false promises:

'These are the things you are to do: Speak the truth to each other, and render true and sound judgment in your courts; do not plot evil against

---

4 For 'covenant', see Prov. 2:17; Ezek. 16:8.

each other, and do not love to swear falsely. I hate all this,' declares the
Lord.
(Zech. 8:16–17)

God hates things that harm us, and God hates actions we do that harm
others. Those who have been discarded by their husbands or wives
because they wanted a replacement spouse or because they wanted a
change will know the immense pain of that kind of divorce, and will be
comforted by knowing that God hates that kind of divorce as well.

b. What should we think about divorce?

In this matter, as in all matters, we should try to think God's thoughts after
him, by studying the Scriptures and believing their teaching. In accepting
God's words, we think his thoughts, and honour him. God values marriage
very highly; so should we. God hates divorce; so we should lament the
premature end of marriages. And we should hate the kind of divorce found
here in Malachi, in which wives were dismissed simply because husbands
wanted to marry other women.

Of course in the Old Testament, although marriage was highly regarded,
divorce was permitted in some limited circumstances (Deut. 24:1–4). In
the New Testament Jesus said that this provision was in place because of
their hard hearts: 'Moses permitted you to divorce your wives because
your hearts were hard' (Matt. 19:8). Jesus also spoke of the priority of
resisting divorce and staying married:

Haven't you read . . . that at the beginning the Creator 'made them male
and female', and said, 'For this reason a man will leave his father and
mother and be united to his wife, and the two will become one flesh'?
So they are no longer two, but one flesh. Therefore what God has joined
together, let no one separate.
(Matt. 19:4–6)

Jesus' priority was to preserve marriages, and to limit unnecessary or
trivial divorces. However, he did allow the possibility of divorce: 'I tell you
that anyone who divorces his wife, except for sexual immorality, and
marries another woman commits adultery' (Matt. 19:9). Paul also allowed
divorce if a believer is married to an unbeliever, and the unbeliever wants
to end the marriage (1 Cor. 7:10–16). Many Christians today hold that

divorce is permitted in these two cases, and none other. Others hold that irretrievable breakdown or domestic violence or abuse are other legitimate grounds for divorce. None believe that marriages should be ended lightly. All would agree that marriage should be honoured, and married couples should be encouraged to stay together. This is more likely to happen if husbands cherish their wives, and wives cherish their husbands, and both husbands and wives work to encourage each other and build up their marriages. It is also more likely to happen if friends support one another in their marriages, and marriage is highly valued in churches.

It remains a serious sin to divorce your wife in order to marry an unbeliever; in such situations, it is clear that God hates divorce, and we too should hate such divorces. As Malachi pointed out, in such cases it is a double sin. It is unfaithfulness: breaking the covenant of marriage, and breaking the covenant unity of God's people.

4. Failing to produce godly offspring (2:15)

God's plan was to produce a great nation from the descendants of Abraham, and that, within the tribes and families, parents would teach their children the law of Moses, show them how to put it into practice, and teach them that the fear of the Lord is the foundation of all wisdom (see Gen. 12:1–3; Exod. 12:21–27; Deut. 6:4–9; Prov. 1 – 7; 31:10–31; Ps. 145:4). To marry a woman who was a worshipper of foreign gods would undermine and imperil this plan. *Judah has desecrated the sanctuary the* LORD *loves by marrying women who worship a foreign god* (11).

By marrying foreigners, Israelite men might well be seduced away from the worship of the Lord as the one true and only God. Their new wives would not be able to teach their children to worship the Lord. The men would have divided hearts, and be less able to teach their children the truth. The extended families of the new wives would influence the children away from the worship of the Lord. The children would have divided loyalties, and might try to worship the gods of their mother as well as the Lord God of their father. The father, mother and children might well try to worship all their family gods, both the Lord God and the other gods as well. Disastrous![5]

---

[5] We find the same problem in Neh. 13:23–27, where the children of mixed marriages could not speak Hebrew, and so would not be able to understand the law of Moses.

There are several ways in which we might apply this message.

First, God loves children being brought up to know and trust the Lord Jesus, and to trust and obey their loving heavenly Father. This is more likely to happen if a believer marries another believer, and they agree to raise their children to know and trust God.

Second, we should encourage Christian parents to pray with their children and pray for them; to teach their children from the Bible; and to model what it means to live as believers.

Third, churches should work hard to support parents in this ministry, and to provide additional mentors for children, and people to train and teach them.

Fourth, as many future believers will not come from the children of believers but from people with no Christian background, churches should be active in evangelism, converting men, women and children to Jesus Christ. The church of Jesus Christ grows by evangelism!

Fifth, the church should warn its members not to flirt with other religions, other ideas, or other ways of living that will seduce people away from pure devotion to Christ. As Paul wrote to the church at Corinth:

> I am jealous for you with a godly jealousy. I promised you to one husband, to Christ, so that I might present you as a pure virgin to him. But I am afraid that just as Eve was deceived by the snake's cunning, your minds may somehow be led astray from your sincere and pure devotion to Christ. For if someone comes to you and preaches a Jesus other than the Jesus we preached, or if you receive a different spirit from the Spirit you received, or a different gospel from the one you accepted, you put up with it easily enough.
> (2 Cor. 11:2–4)

5. Violence (2:16)

We have seen a cluster of sins. The central sin is that Israelite men married women who were idolaters. To do this they had to first divorce their Israelite wives. This meant that they desecrated the holiness of God's temple and God's people. It also meant that their children would be unlikely to grow up knowing and serving the only true God. The other associated sin was that of violence. So Malachi preached: *'The man who hates and divorces his wife,' says the* LORD, *the God of Israel, 'does violence to the one he should protect,' says the* LORD *Almighty. So be on your guard, and do not be unfaithful* (16).

The phrase *does violence* could be translated 'covering one's garment with violence' (see NRSV). What did it mean to cover one's garment with violence? It could mean that violent physical abuse accompanied divorcing a wife. That would of course be appalling. It is, however, more likely to be a reference to the offering of sacrifices. So while the men were divorcing their wives, they were also offering sacrifices in the temple. This links with an earlier verse in this section: *Another thing you do: you flood the* LORD's *altar with tears. You weep and wail because he no longer looks with favour on your offerings or accepts them with pleasure from your hands* (13).

So the men were such hypocrites that they were divorcing their wives and also offering sacrifices, and wondering why the Lord was rejecting them. This was a common problem: continuing to take part in temple worship, while engaging in rank disobedience towards the Lord of the temple. As Micah had prophesied:

> With what shall I come before the LORD
>> and bow down before the exalted God?
> Shall I come before him with burnt offerings,
>> with calves a year old?
> Will the LORD be pleased with thousands of rams,
>> with ten thousand rivers of oil?
> Shall I offer my firstborn for my transgression,
>> the fruit of my body for the sin of my soul?
> He has shown you, O mortal, what is good.
>> And what does the LORD require of you?
> To act justly and to love mercy
>> and to walk humbly with your God?
> (Mic. 6:6–8)

We should remember that hypocrites are usually blind to their hypocrisy. Sin blinds us to sin, and so hypocrisy blinds us to hypocrisy. Hypocrites can rarely see the great gap between their religious practice and their rampant sins. Hypocrisy is usually blind. They just don't see what all the fuss is about. If challenged about their behaviour, they think it is covered by their religious practice. That is why we need good friends to challenge us as individuals. And that is why we need good preachers and leaders of churches to challenge us to repent of our shared hypocrisies as churches.

I remember visiting some friends involved in Christian ministry in a non-Western nation. As they talked about the church there, I became more and more horrified at the sins of that church. When I talked about this with my friends who lived in the country I learnt a lot when they pointed out that churches and Christians are naturally sinful in the ways in which their societies are sinful, and that my strong reaction was against the sins of the culture as much as the sins of the church. They also pointed out that if Christians from that country visited Australia, they would be horrified at the sins of the Australian church, which of course are the sins of Australian society. They kindly suggested that I might be blind to those sins, because they were the sins of my culture! Often we need people from other countries to point out our hypocrisies.

We need to pray that God would do a great miracle and make us single-hearted people, with the purity of heart to desire and will one thing – the glory of God. As Joshua had warned the people of God so long ago of how difficult it was to serve God alone:

> Now fear the LORD and serve him with all faithfulness. Throw away the
> gods your ancestors worshipped beyond the River Euphrates and in
> Egypt, and serve the LORD. But if serving the LORD seems undesirable to
> you, then choose for yourselves this day whom you will serve, whether
> the gods your ancestors served beyond the Euphrates, or the gods of the
> Amorites, in whose land you are living. But as for me and my household,
> we will serve the LORD.
> (Josh. 24:14–15)

6. Pastoral postscript

There are many painful issues raised by this section of Malachi, because marriage and the raising of children are tender issues for many in our churches. Some want to get married, and cannot find someone to marry. Some want to have children, and are not able to do so. Some feel trapped in difficult marriages. Some are married to unbelievers, or to a husband or wife who was formerly a believer but is no longer a practising Christian. Some have raised their children in the faith of Christ, and now find that their children have turned away from Christ. Some have ended their marriages, and now realize that this was a mistake. Some have had children who have died. Some have children who have serious health problems. Some have experienced painful divorce, especially if they have been discarded by their husband or wife. Some have come from very dysfunctional families or marriages, and feel that biblical standards are impossible to achieve. Many feel that their marriages are in a mess. Many parents feel that they are not doing a good job of raising their children. There are people in these situations in most of our churches.

When I meet people in those situations I try to do the following:

- Listen patiently, and try to understand as much as I am able.
- Say, 'Whatever else you do, you should trust God, and trust his love, compassion, power and goodness.'
- Encourage people to find a few good trustworthy and discreet friends to promise to pray for them constantly.
- Say, 'Feel free to tell God all your anger, all your frustration, and all your pain.'
- Pray for them.

I include these comments because some who read this book will be in these painful situations. I also include them to make everyone aware of these personal issues that are present in our churches, and to help people to love those who suffer in these ways. For we should all 'carry each other's burdens, and in this way you will fulfil the law of Christ' (Gal. 6:2). We should do this humbly and with compassion and faithfulness.

These verses from Malachi are a call to faithfulness: a call to be faithful in marriage, a call to be faithful to our fellow believers, and a call to be faithful to our faithful God. To be unfaithful to our fellow believers is to be unfaithful to God. To be unfaithful to the church of Jesus Christ is to be unfaithful to God. We must beware, lest our Judas-hearts lead us to betray others and betray God. God is true to his character that he has revealed to us. He keeps his promises; he is a God of great faithfulness and steadfast covenant love, and his mercies are 'new every morning' and 'never fail' (Lam. 3:22–23). And all God's promises find their 'Yes' in the Lord Jesus Christ (2 Cor. 1:20).

Malachi 2:17 – 3:5

6. Don't weary me

It is a worrying idea that God might weary of the people's words. How had this situation come about? It seems so odd, when we know that God's ears are always open to hear and answer our prayers, but there were many reasons why their words wearied God.

First, God's people had ignored God's words, which meant that their lives were getting further and further away from God's will. They were failing to trust God, love God and obey God. If they had heeded these words of God: 'I have loved you' (1:2), 'where is the honour due to me?' (1:6) and 'you . . . show contempt for my name' (1:6), God would have delighted to hear their words. If they had not been 'unfaithful to one another' (2:10), God would have loved their prayers.

Second, they spoke their words to one another, not to God. They talked about God, complained about God, but did not tell God what was on their hearts or their complaints against him. The book of Psalms includes many complaints against God from individuals and from the people of God, and much questioning of God, his actions and his apparent inactivity (see Pss 3; 5; 7; 10; etc.). On the cross the Lord Jesus cried out, 'My God, my God, why have you forsaken me?' (Matt. 27:46). God does not mind when we address our complaints and questions to him, but he is wearied by our complaining about him.

Third, when they said, *All who do evil are good in the eyes of the LORD, and he is pleased with them*, and *Where is the God of justice?* (2:17), they contradicted the character of God as revealed in his words and his ways. For God delights in those who serve and obey him; and he reigns over heaven and earth to do his purposes.

Fourth, they spread their unbelief to one another and to the community. Not only did they not complain to God, who could bear their complaints, but they complained to one another, and so spread a general mood of unbelief to all. How difficult to say, 'I trust God', when others are complaining about God.

Fifth, this meant that they were failing to do what they should have been doing, that is, encouraging one another in their daily conversations to love God and trust God. They had been told to do this by Moses (Deut. 6:6–9), and shown how to do it in the Psalms:

I will extol the LORD at all times;
  his praise will always be on my lips.
I will glory in the LORD;
  let the afflicted hear and rejoice.
Glorify the LORD with me:
  let us exalt his name together . . .
Taste and see that the LORD is good;
  blessed is the one who takes refuge in him.
(Ps. 34:1–3, 8)

Sixth, they were quite unconscious of what they were doing: *You have wearied the LORD with your words. 'How have we wearied him?' you ask* (2:17). Their repeated sin had blinded them to its presence. All sins blind us, and that is one of the most frightening signs of the present judgment of God. And as our sins weary God (see Isa. 43:22–24), so too our sinful words weary God.

Finally, as we will see in 3:13–15, these words they spoke led them to even stronger words against God.

As we have already seen, failing to do what is right leaves room for doing what is wrong. Failing to take complaints to God led to complaining about God to one another. So also failing to encourage one another led to discouraging one another, and spreading gloom and distrust of God, instead of hope and confidence in him.

I suppose that one of the disadvantages of being God and knowing everything is that you know what people are saying about you! It was certainly not good news at this time. The prevalent mood of God's people was to complain to one another about God, their Lord. They should have turned their grumbles into prayers, and we should do the same. As in our ordinary human relationships, when we have a problem with a person, we should talk to that person about it, not to others. God's saints frequently complain to God, and his ears are always open to their prayers. And he is 'the God of all consolation'; he can console us in all situations and his supply of consolation is infinite (2 Cor. 1:3–7, NRSV).

1. The people's words (2:17)

Let us now pay closer attention to the meaning of their words. We start with *All who do evil are good in the eyes of the Lord, and he is pleased with them* (2:17). They looked around them and they saw people sinning but not being struck down by God. So they assumed that God approved of such sins. They saw the wicked prosper, so they assumed that God delighted in the wicked. Notice that their focus was on others, not on God, and that they envied success. This is a dangerous attitude to have. Those who were sinning and getting away with it were trading on God's patience and forbearance, and those who were observing them were confusing God's patience with God delighting in evil. This was a deep mistake about how God works, and an even deeper mistake about the character of God. Their theological reflection was leading them away from God, not to God, because they were relying on their observation, not on God's self-revelation in Scripture. They should have known that God is a holy God, that he is a patient God, but that he is also a God who judges sin and sinners.

Their other words were, *Where is the God of justice?* By itself, this is a reasonable question, though, as we have seen, only if asked in the context of the prayer, 'Where are you, God of justice?' However, it takes on a darker meaning when seen in the context of what the people had been saying: *All who do evil are good in the eyes of the Lord, and he is pleased with them*. It then becomes clear that this was not a fervent desire for God to act to right wrongs, but instead challenged God's ability or willingness to act. It has the feeling of, 'If he exists, where is he?'

Life would be simpler if God judged all sins immediately. We would know immediately that we had done something wrong or failed to do something right. It would be obvious to the person who had sinned, and obvious to everyone else as well; we might be less likely to do wrong, and more likely to do right. We would never have cause to ask, *Where is the God of justice?* Similarly, if God acted immediately to defend those under attack, to rescue the oppressed, and to reward faith, endurance and sacrifice immediately, life would also be simpler, easier and more straightforward. Waiting for God to act is demanding in many ways.

Why does God make us wait? It is worth commenting that this is an odd question, because it assumes that God should serve us, that God should meet our expectations and our timetable. It assumes that our desires should prevail, and that God is answerable to us. This is not the case, and it is good to recognize that this stance is ridiculous, and to repent of it.

However, the Bible does give us reasons why God waits. God delays his judgment because of his mercy. He wants to give people time to repent. As we have read in Exodus, he is 'The LORD, the LORD, the compassionate and gracious God, slow to anger, and abounding in love and faithfulness' (Exod. 34:6). And as Peter says: 'The Lord is not slow in keeping his promise, as some understand slowness. Instead he is patient with you, not wanting anyone to perish, but everyone to come to repentance' (2 Pet. 3:9). Since the wages of sin is death, if we died in the moment of our sin, we would have no time to repent. So the reason that God delays the return of Christ and his judgment is so that the gospel may be preached, and so that more men, women and children might repent, believe and be saved. This is God's general gospel policy. And it is reflected in the lives of individuals. God bears with our sin, to give us time to repent, to die to sin and to live to righteousness.

And why does God delay in rewarding those who wait for him? The answer is that God wants to train us in enduring faith:

> [You] through faith are shielded by God's power until the coming of the
> salvation that is ready to be revealed in the last time. In all this you
> greatly rejoice, though now for a little while you may have had to suffer
> grief in all kinds of trials. These have come so that the proven
> genuineness of your faith – of greater worth than gold, which perishes
> even though refined by fire – may result in praise, glory and honour
> when Jesus Christ is revealed.
> (1 Pet. 1:5–7)

As we wait on God, our precious faith is being tested. One day it will be gloriously vindicated. We see a great example of this in the Old Testament in the person of Job. God wanted to demonstrate Job's trustworthiness, and let Job suffer in order to do this (Job 1 – 2). We see faith being tested in the whole Old Testament, as all the saints die without having seen all the promises of God fulfilled in the coming of the Lord Jesus Christ. And we see faith being tested in the New Testament and in our own lives, as we wait for the return of Christ in his glory to rescue and transform his people, and to judge the world.[1] As we read the whole Bible on this issue, it is important to remember that the judgments and rewards that God gives his people now are significant in themselves, and also point forward to the eternal judgment and eternal rewards that God will give at the return of Christ.

2. God's response (3:1–5)

We now turn to the message that God gave in response to these complaints and questions. His response is not to appear among them; rather it is to speak to them by means of his prophet. His words are promises of future action: he would send two messengers, to judge and to save. These words were a sufficient reply even though those to whom they were addressed would not see their fulfilment (3:1).

My messenger will prepare God's way, by warning of the coming *Lord* and *messenger of the covenant*. The idea of a messenger to prepare God's way is also found in 4:5–6, where he is identified as the prophet Elijah. The promise of *my messenger* was later fulfilled in the ministry of John the Baptist. Jesus Christ told his disciples of his cousin's identity and ministry, using these words from Malachi: 'This is the one about whom it is written: "I will send my messenger ahead of you, who will prepare your way before you"' (Matt. 11:10).[2]

The second messenger promised is described in these words: *'Then suddenly the Lord you are seeking will come to his temple; the messenger of the covenant, whom you desire, will come,' says the* LORD *Almighty* (1).

This second messenger is both *the Lord* who will *come to his temple*, and also *the messenger of the covenant, whom you desire*. The Lord and this messenger are the same person, as we can see in the following rephrasing of these words:

---

[1] For more on waiting on God, see D. A. Carson, *How Long, O Lord? Reflections on Suffering and Evil* (Nottingham: IVP, 2nd edn 2006).

[2] See also Mark 1:2–3, in which these words from Malachi are combined with words from Isa. 40:3. Here the quotation is introduced as from Isaiah, because he was a greater prophet than Malachi.

He will come suddenly . . . the Lord you are seeking:
The messenger . . . whom you desire will come.[3]

John the Baptist prepared the way for the Lord Jesus Christ, who did come to his temple, and who was the mediator of a new covenant (Heb. 12:24). And Jesus not only visited his temple, he also came to replace it and its sacrifices. In John 2:19–21 we read of the connection between the Jerusalem temple and the body of Christ: ' "Destroy this temple, and I will raise it again in three days" . . . But the temple he had spoken of was his body.'

God in the Lord Jesus Christ will come to save and to judge. This promise was spoken and then written in words so that the people of Malachi's day would understand. The people complained about the absence of God, but they would find his presence challenging: *But who can endure the day of his coming? Who can stand when he appears?* (2), for he would come to refine and purify his priests and his people (2–4).

We find a similar warning in Amos 5:18–20, in which the people desire 'the day of the LORD', but will find it more painful than they anticipate. Such refining will be painful but effective, as we see in the ministry of Jesus Christ to his people when he was on earth. The result will be that the priests (*the Levites*), whose lives and offerings have been condemned (1:6 – 2:9), will now be purified. If the priests and people heed the prophecy, then they will offer acceptable sacrifices, in contrast to their present practice as described in Malachi 1, where they are offering second-rate sacrifices. They had done so before, *as in days gone by, as in former years* (4), presumably referring to the days of Moses and of David. And when the priests are purified, then the people will be purified, so that *the offerings of Judah and Jerusalem will be acceptable to the LORD* (4).

Looking further ahead, we know from Hebrews that the Lord who did come as the mediator of the new covenant was of the tribe of Judah, not of Levi. He was not a levitical priest, but a special priest directly and personally appointed by God to an eternal priesthood, to offer the sacrifice of himself once for all on the cross. The result of his ministry was that all who came to God through him could offer their responsive sacrifices in gratitude for his one sacrifice for sin.

---

3 See Verhoef, *Haggai and Malachi*, p. 288.

Through Jesus, therefore, let us continually offer to God a sacrifice of praise – the fruit of lips that openly profess his name. And do not forget to do good and to share with others, for with such sacrifices God is pleased. (Heb. 13:15–16)

In answer to the question *Where is the God of justice?* (2:17), God replies that he will send a messenger to prepare his way, the messenger of the covenant. In answer to the grumble *All who do evil are good in the eyes of the LORD, and he is pleased with them*, he tells them that the evil will certainly be judged (3:5).

They are asking, 'Why does God not act?' God's question is, 'Are you ready for my coming?' The evidence shows that they do not fear God since they treat others badly, they practise sorcery, they commit adultery, they bear false witness, they pay unfair wages, and they do not provide for widows, orphans, outsiders and refugees.

We may wonder at God's patience with evil people. But of course we praise him for his patience with ourselves! And we must remember that, as Peter tells us:

with the Lord a day is like a thousand years, and a thousand years are like a day . . . But in keeping with his promise we are looking forward to a new heaven and a new earth, where righteousness dwells.

So then, dear friends, since you are looking forward to this, make every effort to be found spotless, blameless and at peace with him. Bear in mind that our Lord's patience means salvation. (2 Pet. 3:8, 13–15)

Malachi 3:6–12

7. Return to me, don't rob me

The people have accused God of inconstancy and of unreliability (2:17). They are in a downward spiral; they doubt God's love, so they respond with inadequate sacrifices, inadequate ministry and unfaithfulness in marriage, distrust of God's rule and general injustice in the community, as we have seen in 1:1 – 3:5. They blame God for their problems with God. They blame God, and do not see that they are punishing him. They blame God, and do not see their sin. They blame God, and do not accept his words. We see this in the familiar pattern in this book of God's statement, their rejection of what God says, and God's provision of evidence to support his statement, as in 1:2; 1:6–7; 2:17.

They have not had the nerve to abandon God; it is more like an unhappy marriage than a divorce! God's remedy for this broken relationship is for his people to turn to him, just as he turns to them.

1. 'I do not change' (3:6)

The people complain about God's inconsistency, but in fact he remains the same. That is why they still exist as his people: *I the Lord do not change. So you, the descendants of Jacob, are not destroyed* (6). It is significant that God addresses them as *descendants of Jacob*. They are physically descendants of those three generations of patriarchs: Abraham, Isaac and Jacob. However, God has already pointed to his electing and covenant love in choosing Jacob instead of his older brother Esau (1:2). Their existence as God's people depends on the choice and election of God, for 'God's gifts and his call are irrevocable' (Rom. 11:29; and see Rom. 9:6–15; 11:1–32).

They complain about the character of God, and take their revenge on him by petty acts of disobedience, but in fact their only hope lies in the character and constancy of God. Without him, they are nothing. *I . . . do not change. So you . . . are not destroyed.*

So too our only hope lies in God's electing love in Christ:

> For those God foreknew he also predestined to be conformed to the image of his Son, that he might be the firstborn among many brothers and sisters. And those he predestined, he also called; those he called, he also justified; those he justified, he also glorified.
> (Rom. 8:29–30)

As Paul shows us in Romans 8, it is this electing love of God in Christ that is the basis of our confidence that nothing 'will be able to separate us from the love of God that is in Christ Jesus our Lord' (Rom. 8:39). God had remained the same, yet *Ever since the time of your ancestors you have turned away from my decrees and have not kept them* (7).

It is disturbing that God's people were currently turning away from him; it is even more disturbing that this behaviour had been characteristic of them for generations. This is not a one-off falling away. Its roots lie deep within them, and it is typical, even 'normal' behaviour.

2. Robbing God (3:7–9)

Yet despite their continued tendency to turn aside from God's ways, God still calls on them to return to him. *'Return to me, and I will return to you,' says the Lord Almighty* (7). God's love is electing love, constant love, faithful love, generous love, forgiving love, everlasting love, challenging love, promising love and hopeful love. You *return to me, and I will return to you.* God is constantly working to restore, maintain and strengthen his relationship with his people, and constantly calling on his people to return to him, and maintain and strengthen their relationship with him.

However, they show how far they have fallen by asking, *How are we to return?* This might have been a genuine question, coming from a deep desire for reconciliation. In the light of the message of Malachi as a whole, and in the light of their characteristic response to God's previous words in this prophecy, I suspect it is more like, 'We have no idea that we have done anything wrong, no idea that we have turned away from you, and no idea of needing to do anything to return to you'! They don't know how far they are from God. This suspicion is reinforced by the next words of God and of the people. God says, *Will a mere mortal rob God? Yet you rob me.* And the people reply, *How are we robbing you?* (8). Their words of surprise and ignorance reveal how far they are away from God, how unconscious of his expectations, and how unbelieving of his words.

Robbing God is an extraordinary idea! It seems a ridiculous activity. Yet the early nineteenth-century preacher Charles Simeon once began a sermon based on this text in this way: 'Will a man rob God? Yet you have all robbed him! You!, and you!!, and you!!!'[1]

We rob God when we do not give him what we owe him. We owe him our trust, our love, our service, our obedience, our worship and our sacrifice. We owe him ourselves. And we owe him because he made us, and because he redeemed us in Christ: 'You are not your own; you were bought at a price' (1 Cor. 6:19–20).

> For you know that it was not with perishable things such as silver or gold that you were redeemed from the empty way of life handed down to you from your ancestors, but with the precious blood of Christ, a lamb without blemish or defect.
> (1 Pet. 1:18–19)

How were God's people robbing God in Malachi's day? *In tithes and offerings. You are under a curse – your whole nation – because you are robbing me* (8–9). So it was not just the priests who were offering second-rate sacrifices (1:6–14). The contagion had spread to all the people, who were treating God in the same way in their tithes and offerings – and it was the whole nation which was robbing God. When everyone is committing a sin, when the leaders are committing the same sin, it is very difficult for one person to stand out against it. If anyone decided that he or she would not rob God in the tithe or offering, that person would be hated by others, because the sins of the many would be shown up by the righteousness of the one. Sinners always hate those who don't commit the same sin, because it brings their guilt home to them. So what a great tragedy it was that God had to say, *your whole nation . . . you are robbing me.*

---

[1] H. E. Hopkins, *Charles Simeon of Cambridge* (London: Hodder & Stoughton, 1977), p. 63.

The tithes and offerings were the way in which they provided financial support for the temple, the priests and Levites, the services of the temple, and the poor and needy in the community. Robbing the temple, and robbing the poor and needy, was robbing God.

The idea of robbing God also shows that the people had the wrong idea about their property and possessions. They thought that they owned what they had, whereas in fact they were God's stewards of all their 'possessions', as indeed we are God's stewards of our 'possessions'. As Peter Craigie wrote, 'Their attitude towards property was not one of stewardship, according to which their possessions were held as a sacred trust from God, but was one of ownership.'[2]

If we think we own all we have, then we are naturally reluctant to part with any of it. If we think that God owns all we have, then we are free to give it away on his behalf. And, ironically, we will value what we keep for ourselves more highly, because it is a personal gift of our gracious God to us. Being God's steward to give or to keep is an immense privilege. We see in the people of Malachi's day the dire results of being possessed by possessions.

In addition to all of this, we can see that the people made the easy mistake of valuing the gifts of God more than God the giver of the gifts. So when they did not get the gifts they wanted, they turned against the giver. We try to teach children to pay more attention to the people who give them gifts than to the gifts themselves. Perhaps we still have to learn the same lesson!

And what is the result of robbing God? *You are under a curse – your whole nation – because you are robbing me.* This curse of God is the opposite of his blessing. God chose Abraham to bless him and to bless the great nation that would be his descendants. But great blessing brings great responsibility, and great blessing and great responsibility bring the possibility of great judgment. Read Deuteronomy 28 – 30 for that great moment of clarity when Moses put before the people the two options of God's blessing or God's curse. The curse of God comes on his people when they break God's covenant, distrust God's word, disobey his commands, reject his love, distrust his promises, reject his messengers, and fail to love and serve him alone. It is a striking fact that the book of Malachi ends with God's warning: 'or else I will come and strike the land with total destruction' (4:6).

---

[2] Craigie, *Twelve Prophets*, p. 242.

The seriousness of this curse of God can be seen very clearly when we realize that the only way the accumulated curse of God on his people could be finally lifted was through the death of the Lord Jesus on the cross:

> Christ redeemed us from the curse of the law by becoming a curse for us, for it is written: 'Cursed is everyone who is hung on a pole.' He redeemed us in order that the blessing given to Abraham might come to the Gentiles through Christ Jesus, so that by faith we might receive the promise of the Spirit.
> (Gal. 3:13–14)

What was the temporary remedy in Malachi's day? *Bring the whole tithe into the storehouse . . . and see if I will not throw open the floodgates of heaven* (10–12). Here was the irony of the situation. They no doubt used their poverty as a reason for robbing God in their tithes and offerings, thinking, 'Well, if God is going to be stingy towards us, then we will be stingy towards him!' But in fact, as they should have known from Deuteronomy 28 – 30, their poverty was a warning from God that all was not well in their relationship with him. Their poverty was in fact a loving warning, in the same way in which God disciplines those he loves even today (Heb. 12:3–13). But his people took it as an excuse for taking revenge on God.

3. 'Put me to the test' (3:10–12)

In these verses we find God calling and challenging his people, his generous offer to them and his promise. God wanted to bless them, and invited them to receive his rich and effective blessings.

First, he calls his people to *bring the whole tithe into the storehouse*, and challenges them to *test me in this* (10). He offers to *open the floodgates of heaven and pour out so much blessing that there will not be room enough to store it*, and to protect their produce from harm by *prevent[ing] pests from devouring your crops, and the vines in your fields* (11). Finally God makes a promise: *'Then all the nations will call you blessed, for yours will be a delightful land,' says the Lord Almighty* (12).

The visible sign of God's blessing was prosperity, as the visible sign of his curse was poverty. Is this still true in our day? Should we teach people that if they obey God they will be prosperous, and that if they are poor then they must be disobeying God?

Let's think a bit more about life for followers of God in the Old Testament. First, poverty and riches have a variety of meanings. Poverty might be a sign of the righteous person being persecuted (for example, in Ps. 70), or of a righteous person having his or her trust in God tested, as in the case of Job (Job 1 – 2; 42). So although poverty might be a sign of covenant disobedience, it might also have another meaning. Similarly, riches were not always a sign of obedience. Rich people were often opposed to God, and oppressed others (Ps. 73). We must learn not to universalize one passage from the Bible and think that it tells us all we need to know on a subject. We need to know our Bibles well, so that we know what other passages of the Bible need to be taken into account, and then decide which passage applies most directly to a current situation. For it would be a disaster for poor righteous people to think that their poverty represented the curse of God, as it would be a disaster for arrogant wealthy people to think that their wealth meant that God approved of their behaviour.

Second, Proverbs warns of the dangers of both wealth and poverty:

> Give me neither poverty nor riches,
>   but give me only my daily bread.
> Otherwise, I may have too much and disown you
>   and say, 'Who is the LORD?'
> Or I may become poor and steal,
>   and so dishonour the name of my God.
> (Prov. 30:8–9)

Third, the New Testament tells us that Old Testament believers were not as focused on temporal earthly blessings as we might think. We read in Hebrews 11 that some of those Old Testament believers 'were longing for a better country – a heavenly one. Therefore God is not ashamed to be called their God, for he has prepared a city for them' (Heb. 11:16). So even in the Old Testament, people knew that their present blessings were only a foretaste and promise of greater future blessings. Great blessings were promises of a greater future, as curses were warnings of the future final judgment of God.

We too need to learn from our present circumstances by reflecting on them in the light of all that the Bible teaches us about the ways of God. And we too need to learn to wait for the return of Christ for his assessment of us and our lives, and for our future rewards of grace.

I recently came across a saying from the seventeenth-century preacher Thomas Brooks. He was obviously a generous preacher, because his nickname was 'Babbling Brooks'! He said, 'Two things are very rare: the one is, to see a young man humble and watchful; and the other is, to see an old man contented and cheerful.'[3] The striking reality is that the people of God in Malachi's day were neither humble nor contented. The other striking reality is God's constancy and patience in sending his prophet Malachi to encourage them to return to their God, and to stop robbing him.

3 'Apples of Gold by Thomas Brooks, 1660', Chapter 3: 'The Evils of Youth', <http://www.gracegems.org/Brooks/apples_of_gold3.htm>, accessed 25 August 2012.

Malachi 3:13 – 4:6

8. Final words

We come to the last section of Malachi. It includes the final words of God's people who are refusing to receive God's words (3:13–15); a reference to the words spoken by some of God's people who did revere his words, and God's words about them (3:16–18); and the final words of God, both words of warning and words of comfort (4:1–6).

1. Don't say harsh things against me (3:13–15)

'You have spoken arrogantly against me,' says the LORD. 'Yet you ask, "What have we said against you?"' (13). Here is a familiar pattern of interaction between God and his people, in which God speaks of what the people are doing wrong, and they deny it. It is worth reminding ourselves that the people have done the same with God's previous words (see 1:2–3, 6–14; 2:13–14, 17; 3:7–9).

We see three important things about the people, which reiterate what has gone before. First, they are unconscious of their many sins. Second, they automatically disbelieve, question and contradict God. And third, they are slow to learn, as they keep on making the same mistake, committing the same sin of doubting God's words. It looks farcical and almost hard to believe that they could be so blind, if it were not that these responses to God occur again and again in every generation of God's people in the pages of the Bible, and in all ages, including our own, and in all places, including our churches and our hearts. Yet God persists, as shown by his sending of his prophet Malachi to his people long ago, and as shown in his using these same words of his prophet Malachi to speak to us today, and to call us to return to him.

It is also significant that these *arrogant* words against the Lord seem to be a more extreme version of those Lord-wearying words of 2:17. They obviously did not heed the warning in chapter 2, or they would not have needed the more severe warning of chapter 3! They were persisting in their malicious and defamatory gossip about God, for these are *arrogant* words *against me* (13). Again, as in 2:17, they are not addressing the Lord to his face, but spreading lies about him. Because they do not understand and make the obvious connections between God's words and their words, God reminds them of what they have been saying (14–15).

They sound to me like those who grumbled in the desert in the time of Moses (Num. 11:1–35 and 14:1–4). Actually they sound like grumblers against God in every age: and there are even echoes in our own hearts and sometimes on our own lips.

What do we gain . . . ? (14) is such a revealing question! It shows that they are fundamentally self-centred, not God-centred. This is the embarrassing question that occasionally comes to us midway through our lives as Christians, and the painful question that can come near the end of years of ministry. What have I got out of all of this? Have the sacrifices been worthwhile? What reward do I have for my goodness and service of God? In particular the people complain, *What do we gain by carrying out his requirements and going about like mourners before the* Lord *Almighty?* Keeping God's commands has not brought them any benefit, and neither has their penitence when they have failed to keep them. Whatever they have done, they feel that they are the losers.

If the words *What do we gain . . . ?* reveal so much about their deep and destructive motivation, the following words reveal much about their deep and destructive tendency to envy those who have not even bothered to keep God's commands or to sorrow for their sins. *Now we call the arrogant blessed. Certainly evildoers prosper, and even when they put God to the test, they get away with it* (15). Envying other people's happiness is fatal to our confidence in God. Distant fields are always greener. But more to the point, God's people here are envying those who are openly and successfully *arrogant*. They did not have the nerve to be wholeheartedly arrogant against God, so instead they envy those who are arrogant. For those arrogant people not only prosper, but *when they put God to the test, they get away with it*. What revealing words these are! Those who were speaking harsh words against God envied those who put God to the test and got away with it.

Whereas God's invitation to 'test me in this' in 3:10 is an invitation to repent and trust God for his promised blessings, this putting God to the test in 3:15 is seeing how much you can get away with in disobeying God. It is the behaviour of arrogant people. Of course, what those who complain fail to see is that when God lets people get away with it, that is actually a form of judgment. As we have already observed, murder not only hurts the person who is killed, it also hurts the murderer, because, having got away with one murder, that person then thinks that he or she is clever enough to get away with another. God is patient with sinners; he does not strike us down dead the moment we sin. He is patient because he wants to give us time to repent and be forgiven. But his patience is also risky, because it might make us think that sin does not matter, and it might make others think that they can get away with the same sin. This is often how sins spread in a community.

I have heard words like *What do we gain . . . ?* many times on the lips of obedient but discontented believers, and I have also heard words of regret and envy like *Now we call the arrogant blessed.* So often in our experience it feels as though it has been futile to serve God, because those who do so are not rewarded, and those who don't serve God seem to have more fun and get away with it. How sad to hear and see embittered goodness and godliness, often in faithful Christian people. And these words echo the sentiments of 2:17, 'Where is the God of justice?', because it seems so unjust of God to treat his servants so badly, and to let others enjoy themselves so much!

It is worth pointing out that ministers are particularly prone to envy of other ministers, and they find it more difficult if they have sacrificed much in order to do their ministry, and yet see others who are more 'successful' in ministry. Here are some ways in which I try to help people begin to shift such a painful logjam. It needs time and patience to do this, because the pain is so deep.

Comparing ourselves with others will always leave us either discontented or arrogant. It is an unhealthy approach to life, and always makes us unhappy. We can choose people who have more than we have, and this will make us discontented. We can choose people who have less than we do, and this will make us arrogant. Comparisons are odious!

We should focus instead on our relationship with God. We are all more naturally inclined to think about what God has *not given* us or has *not done* for us, as well as about all that *we have done* for God. Spend some time each day for two weeks praising God for every good gift that he has given you, small or great.

Envy blinds us to the difficulties that others face, even those whom we envy. If we knew the truth about their lives, we might have less cause to be envious. We live in a world of inequalities: do these inequalities matter so much that you would let them destroy you? Yes, sinners do get away with blue murder. But God is patient with you when you sin, even the sin of envy.

You are here to serve God: God is not here to serve you! You will never be content if you compare yourself with others, and you are the only person who can stop yourself doing it. Don't blame others for your attitude to them. Envy is the enemy of contentment. The irony is that the people you envy are those who have learnt not to envy others: you will never get what you want.

We betray our inmost selves by our words and actions. Malachi's people robbed God (3:8–10), and they spoke harsh words of resentment against God (3:13–15). This shows that they were fundamentally self-centred, not God-centred, that they were selfish at a very deep level, rather than worshipping and serving God alone. They had made idols of themselves, and so failed to honour God. They wanted their own glory, not God's glory. I once read this ancient saying: 'Too covetous is he for whom God is not enough.'[1] We need to learn to be content with God, even when God does not serve us as we want.

Being self-centred is one of the curses of our age. It is hard for two self-centred people to sustain a marriage. Self-centred parents find children very demanding. Self-centred children find it hard to honour their father and mother. Self-centred people find belonging to a church very challenging, and churches find it challenging to cope with self-centred people. Self-centred people are out for what they can get in their workplace, in their local community, in their nation and in their world. And self-centred people find it hard to cope with God, who will not serve them as they want.

The people in Malachi's day looked as if they were serving God, and thought they were serving God, at least as much as he deserved. In fact they were serving themselves, and were angry that God would not do the same.

---

[1] Quoted in A. Huxley, *Grey Eminence: A Study in Religion and Politics* (London: Chatto & Windus, 1944), p. 33.

2. They will be mine (3:16–18)

Here are some more final words. They are the words that are spoken to one another by *those who feared the LORD* (16). And then we have the words the Lord spoke about these people: *they will be my treasured possession* (17).

This is the first time we have read of a positive response to the words of the Lord through the prophet Malachi. To this point the response has all been negative, as the people have doubted, questioned and rejected God's words. But as at all times among God's people, there is a 'remnant', those within the people of God who do respond to God's words with faith and obedience. They are those who *feared*, or 'revered', *the LORD* (16).

We read in Proverbs that 'The fear of the LORD is the beginning of wisdom' (Prov. 9:10). Fearing God, respecting God, reverencing God, is the first step in wisdom and the true foundation of wisdom. Let's learn wisdom. Of course we would prefer it if we could eradicate sin with positive motivations and reasons, such as loving God, or seeking God's glory. But God provides negative motivations for us as well as positive motivations, because we need both.

To be honest, we all need fear to drive some sins from our lives. What stops me (mostly) from driving over the speed limit? It's the fear of speed cameras, fines, demerit points and losing my driver's licence. Someone put $200 in my hand when I began ministry, saying, 'For the church.' What stopped me taking $20 for myself, on the basis that I had worked very hard over the last week? It was the fear that if I took $20 now, I would find a good reason to take the lot in a few years' time in similar circumstances, and that my ministry would be destroyed. What keeps me from secret sins, which are so easy for a single person? It is the knowledge that one day I will have to give an account for my life and ministry to the Lord Jesus. We need to learn a healthy fear of God.

Jesus mostly called people to receive good gifts. But sometimes he warned people of the danger they were in because of the judgment of God, for example in the parable of the tenants (Matt. 21:33–44), and in his warnings to the Pharisees and teachers of the law in Matthew 23:1–36. In the parable of the sheep and the goats he encouraged the sheep with the promise of eternal life and warned the goats of eternal punishment (Matt. 25:31–46).

And notice that when Jesus was teaching his disciples in Luke 12 he gave three instructions about fear. They are: don't fear those who can only

hurt your bodies; fear God who can throw you into hell, 'Yes . . . fear him';
and don't be afraid of God, because you are worth more than many
sparrows. This last instruction is reinforced later: his followers should not
be afraid, 'for your Father has been pleased to give you the kingdom' (Luke
12:4–5, 7, 32).

At first sight it looks a bit confusing to be told to fear God and then not
fear God. The first is meant to deliver us from fearing people, for the worst
they can do is kill us, whereas God can send us to hell. But we should not
fear him, because he cares for us, and will give us his kingdom.

We find similar themes in Psalm 34. God delivers us from fears, and
protects those who fear him:

> I sought the LORD, and he answered me;
>> he delivered me from all my fears . . .
> The angel of the LORD encamps around those who fear him,
>> and he delivers them.
> (Ps. 34:4, 7)

Paradoxically, we need not fear God's love, as long as we fear his judgment.
Those who find refuge in him have no need to fear him (Ps. 2:12).

Not only did these good people fear God, they also encouraged one
another: *Then those who feared the LORD talked with each other* (16). God
has made us for positive relationships with one another, and a vital part
of those relationships is mutual encouragement. We need to be encouraged by others, and we need to encourage others as well. Encouragement
is a good mixture of personal interest, affirmation of what is good
and godly, exhortation to continue, endure and grow, warning of any
dangers, and promise of support, interest, love and prayers. It is a mutual
ministry to which all are called, and which all need. No wonder Hebrews
tells us:

> Encourage one another daily, as long as it is called 'Today', so that none
> of you may be hardened by sin's deceitfulness. We have come to share in
> Christ, if indeed we hold our original conviction firmly to the very end.
> (Heb. 3:13–14)

> And let us consider how we may spur one another on towards love and
> good deeds, not giving up meeting together, as some are in the habit of

doing, but encouraging one another – and all the more as you see the Day approaching.
(Heb. 10:24–25)

In Malachi's day the people who responded to God's words through the prophet also encouraged one another to fear God and so have a heart able to receive his words. And notice God's response to them, as he listened and then spoke: *And the* LORD *listened and heard. A scroll of remembrance was written in his presence concerning those who feared the* LORD *and honoured his name . . . 'They will be my treasured possession'* (16–17).

How much the Lord values those who revere or fear him, and who think on his name, his revelation of himself! A *scroll of remembrance* records their names, making clear their importance to God. The Lord affirms, *They will be my treasured possession.* The whole people of God were called to belong to God:

Now if you obey me fully and keep my covenant, then out of all nations you will be my treasured possession. Although the whole earth is mine, you will be for me a kingdom of priests and a holy nation.
(Exod. 19:5–6)

This idea is echoed in Psalm 135:4: 'For the LORD has chosen Jacob to be his own, Israel to be his treasured possession.' Remember that it is some, not all of the people, who have this honour. There is 'a remnant chosen by grace' (Rom. 11:5). As the names of this faithful remnant were written in God's book of remembrance, so too their names will be included with all the saints among those written in 'the Lamb's book of life' (Rev. 21:27). This is a forward-focused action of God. *'On the day when I act,' says the* LORD *Almighty, 'they will be my treasured possession. I will spare them, just as a father has compassion and spares his son who serves him'* (17).

The day when God will act is the day of the Lord, the day of judgment, the day when God would rescue and vindicate his people, when the wicked would be judged, and when all would see the separation between the righteous and the wicked. *And you will again see the distinction between the righteous and the wicked, between those who serve God and those who do not* (18). On that day, no-one will say, 'All who do evil are good in the eyes of the LORD, and he is pleased with them', or 'Where is the God of justice?' (2:17). On that day, no-one will say,

> *It is futile to serve God. What do we gain by carrying out his requirements and going about like mourners before the LORD Almighty? But now we call the arrogant blessed. Certainly evildoers prosper, and even when they put God to the test, they get away with it.*
> (3:14–15)

The day of the Lord will be God's final reply, his final vindication, and his final word.

3. The day of the Lord (4:1–3)

What will that day be like? What will it achieve? The first answer in Malachi 4 is that it will be a day that burns like an oven, on which the arrogant and evildoers will be burnt up:

> *'Surely the day is coming; it will burn like a furnace. All the arrogant and every evildoer will be stubble, and that day that is coming will set them on fire,' says the LORD Almighty. 'Not a root or a branch will be left to them.'*
> (1)

Those arrogant people, previously envied (3:15), will now be judged. God had previously refined his people: now he will finally judge them.

The second answer is that it is the day on which the sun will rise with righteousness and healing: *But for you who revere my name, the sun of righteousness will rise with healing in its rays* (2).

The day will dawn with the rising of the sun of righteousness, and its rays will bring healing and comfort for those who fear God, revere him and think on his name. We read in Isaiah of the servant of the Lord, 'the punishment that brought us peace was on him, and by his wounds we are healed' (Isa. 53:5); and Peter writes of the suffering of the Lord Jesus who 'bore our sins in his body on the cross . . . by his wounds you have been healed' (1 Pet. 2:24). That forgiveness and healing achieved on the cross will finally have its full effect when Christ returns in glory, and we will be raised. It will be a day of righteousness:

But the day of the Lord will come like a thief. The heavens will disappear with a roar; the elements will be destroyed by fire, and the earth and everything done in it will be laid bare.

Since everything will be destroyed in this way, what kind of people ought you to be? You ought to live holy and godly lives as you look forward to the day of God and speed its coming. That day will bring about the destruction of the heavens by fire, and the elements will melt in the heat. But in keeping with his promise we are looking forward to a new heaven and a new earth, where righteousness dwells.
(2 Pet. 3:10–13)

This is that final separation of which we read in Psalm 1: 'For the LORD watches over the way of the righteous, but the way of the wicked leads to destruction' (Ps. 1:6). And it is the final separation that Jesus foretold in his parable of the wise man and the foolish man.

Therefore everyone who hears these words of mine and puts them into practice is like a wise man who built his house on the rock. The rain came down, the streams rose, and the winds blew and beat against that house; yet it did not fall, because it had its foundation on the rock. But everyone who hears these words of mine and does not put them into practice is like a foolish man who built his house on sand. The rain came down, the streams rose, and the winds blew and beat against that house, and it fell with a great crash.
(Matt. 7:24–27)

In Moses' day there were fundamentally two ways to live: under the blessing of God, or under the curse of God. In Malachi's day there were two ways to live: receiving God's words through the prophet, or rejecting God's words through the prophet. In Christ's day there were two ways to live: hearing and acting on Christ's words, or hearing them and not acting on them. So today there are two ways to live: following God or rejecting God.

These verses raise three difficult issues.

The first is the judgment of God on the ungodly and arrogant people. How can a God of love condemn people finally and irrevocably? The answer lies in the fact that God is the judge as well as the saviour. For 'God is love', but it is also true that 'God is light' (1 John 4:16; 1:5). And Jesus Christ spoke clearly of the reality of hell, and warned people to stay out of it (e.g. Matt. 25:46; Mark 9:42–48; Luke 12:5). It is an aspect of the awful dignity and responsibility we bear as humans made in the image of God that our actions are significant and powerful, that we have to face the consequences of our actions, and that our actions have consequences for eternity as well as in time. The fact is that we all deserve the fires of hell, and only the saving death of Christ can rescue us from that judgment. So Paul wrote to the Thessalonians, and reminded them of 'how you turned to God from idols to serve the living and true God, and to wait for his Son from heaven, whom he raised from the dead – Jesus, who rescues us from the coming wrath' (1 Thess. 1:9–10).

The second difficult issue is of the nature of the fate of the ungodly. Do they suffer eternally, or are they destroyed? Malachi 4:1 seems to teach that they will be destroyed, or burnt up:

'Surely the day is coming; it will burn like a furnace. All the arrogant and every evildoer will be stubble, and that day that is coming will set them on fire,' says the Lord Almighty. 'Not a root or a branch will be left to them.'

If we want to think through this question, then we need to look at all the biblical evidence, especially in the New Testament. When we go to the New Testament we need to clarify the question of the fate of the ungodly. For at the general resurrection of all people on the day when the Lord Jesus Christ returns, everyone will be raised, good and evil alike. As Christ taught,

a time is coming when all who are in their graves will hear his voice and come out – those who have done what is good will rise to live, and those who have done what is evil will rise to be condemned.
(John 5:28–29)

So everyone will be raised, with resurrection bodies – some to life, and some to condemnation (see also Rom. 14:10–12; 2 Cor. 5:10; Rev. 20:11–15). Those who trust in Jesus as 'the resurrection and the life', who live and believe in him, 'will never die' (John 11:25–26). So they will live for eternity with Christ. What about those who are not saved? The two options are that either they do stay alive for eternity in their resurrection bodies, though separated from God, or that after the judgment they are annihilated. One difficulty in resolving this issue is that much of the language used to communicate what will happen is picture language, like that of fire burning up stubble or chaff in Malachi 4:1. My own view is that punishment is eternal, as God made humans so that our decisions and actions in our lifetimes have eternal consequences.

The third difficult issue is what to make of the promise in Malachi 4 that the righteous will tread down the wicked. We read: *'You will go out and frolic like well-fed calves. Then you will trample on the wicked; they will be ashes under the soles of your feet on the day when I act,' says the* Lord *Almighty* (2–3).

Whatever we make of this, it does not provide any justification for our taking revenge on those who persecute us for our Christian beliefs or actions. Paul wrote: 'Bless those who persecute you; bless and do not curse . . . Do not take revenge, my dear friends, but leave room for God's wrath, for it is written: "It is mine to avenge; I will repay," says the Lord' (Rom. 12:14, 19). If we are persecuted, we hope that the government will protect us (Rom. 13:1–4). If our government does not protect us, then we must follow Christ's example and entrust ourselves to God who judges justly (1 Pet. 2:21–23).

This continues to be an issue for many believers throughout the world today. If we are not facing it ourselves at present, we should pay attention, because it may happen to us in the future. And we should also pay attention so that we are better able to pray for persecuted brothers and sisters in Christ.

Back to Malachi 4:2–3. What about that idea of enjoying revenge we find here – is that a Christian idea? Paul writes of the final vindication of God and of God's people in 2 Thessalonians. The situation is that the believers at Thessalonica are being severely persecuted, and at the same time Paul and his ministry companions are also enduring persecution. So Paul writes:

Therefore, among God's churches we boast about your perseverance and faith in all the persecutions and trials you are enduring.

All this is evidence that God's judgment is right, and as a result you will be counted worthy of the kingdom of God, for which you are suffering. God is just: he will pay back trouble to those who trouble you and give relief to you who are troubled, and to us as well. This will happen when the Lord Jesus is revealed from heaven in blazing fire with his powerful angels. He will punish those who do not know God

and do not obey the gospel of our Lord Jesus. They will be punished
with everlasting destruction and shut out from the presence of the
Lord and from the glory of his might on the day he comes to be glorified
in his holy people and to be marvelled at among all those who have
believed. This includes you, because you believed our testimony
to you.
(2 Thess. 1:4–10)

These are strong words! They do make it clear that God will make the
punishment fit the crime, and will 'pay back trouble to those who trouble
you'. I find these words of great comfort when I think of those countless
believers today and in the history of Christianity who have suffered persecution, privation, torture and death for the sake of Christ, and who have
endured watching their families and friends suffering the same afflictions
for Christ's sake. I want God to reward them. I want God to avenge them.
I want God to make unmistakably clear to their persecutors the awful
things they have done. I remember the words of John Paton, one of the first
missionaries to Vanuatu, then called New Hebrides. When facing death,
he said to his attacker, 'If you kill me, God will judge you!' An appropriate
warning: God will vindicate his people.

Is this a Christian view? Well, Paul was an apostle of the risen Christ,
a spokesman for Christ. And Christ himself gave a solemn warning to the
scribes and Pharisees who opposed him:

Woe to you, teachers of the law and Pharisees, you hypocrites! You build
tombs for the prophets and decorate the graves of the righteous. And
you say, 'If we had lived in the days of our ancestors, we would not have
taken part with them in shedding the blood of the prophets.' So you
testify against yourselves that you are the descendants of those who
murdered the prophets. Go ahead, then, and complete what your
ancestors started!
    You snakes! You brood of vipers! How will you escape being
condemned to hell?
(Matt. 23:29–33)

When we find Bible teaching which we find hard to accept, it is worth
remembering the saying of Augustine of Hippo, an early church leader: 'If
you believe what you like in the Gospels, and reject what you don't like, it

is not the gospel you believe, but yourself.'[2] We should delight in the perfection of God's coming kingdom and glory.

4. God's final words (4:4–6)

God's final words in this book of Malachi point back to Moses, and forward to the coming of Elijah. In the Old Testament, Moses and Elijah were important prophets. Moses was associated with the law, and Elijah with the prophets. Moses was the first prophet, and Malachi was the last prophet of Old Testament times.

So God points the people back to Moses' teaching: *Remember the law of my servant Moses, the decrees and laws I gave him at Horeb for all Israel* (4).[3] In this context, the word *remember* means to keep in mind and put into practice. All the prophets in different ways applied the law of Moses to the people of God in their day, and urged them to keep it, to remember it, to trust it and to practise it. If the people of God in Malachi's day had remembered the law of Moses, there would have been no need for Malachi's ministry! If the people want to continue to be God's people, then they must heed this imperative, and remember the teaching of Moses. Looking back to the words God has spoken in the past is a feature of faith and obedience in the Old Testament as it is in the New Testament. And as they were told to remember Moses' teaching, so are we. For Moses 'received living words to pass on to us' (Acts 7:38), and 'these things . . . were written down as warnings for us, on whom the culmination of the ages has come' (1 Cor. 10:11). We remember the teaching of Moses and the prophets, as we also receive the teaching of Jesus Christ and his apostles in the New Testament. It may seem an odd thing to do, but as we look back in history to see the saving works of God in the Old Testament and in God's Son, the Lord Jesus Christ, and his death and resurrection, so we look back in history to hear the saving words of God in Old and New Testament alike, as they point us to Christ, who brings us to God.

First God points back to Moses, then he points forward to Elijah:

See, I will send the prophet Elijah to you before that great and dreadful day of the LORD comes. He will turn the hearts of the parents to their

---

[2] Paraphrase of Augustine, *Contra Faustum* 17.3, New Advent, <http://www.newadvent.org/fathers/140617.htm>, accessed 23 August 2012.

[3] Horeb is another name for Mount Sinai.

children, and the hearts of the children to their parents; or else I will come
and strike the land with total destruction.
(5–6)

God had sent Elijah at a very low point in the history of the people of God, when most had deserted God, and those who continued to serve God were very discouraged (see 1 Kgs 17 – 2 Kgs 2). Elijah had a lonely and tempestuous ministry, but stood firm for God in the church and in the nation.

God tells his people that he will send Elijah, to call them to repentance. What should we make of this promise? Some believed that Elijah would indeed come again, and there are references to this in the Gospels. Some thought that Jesus was Elijah (Mark 8:28), and some thought that Jesus called for Elijah to come and rescue him at his crucifixion (Mark 15:35).

Was John the Baptist Elijah? He certainly came with an Elijah-like ministry, calling God's people to repentance (Luke 1:67–79; 3:1–18). John is described with words from Malachi 3:1, 'I will send my messenger, who will prepare the way before me', in Mark 1:3 and Matthew 11:10, and Jesus told his disciples that if they were willing to receive it, John 'is the Elijah who was to come' (Matt. 11:14). And we read in Luke 1:17 that John came 'in the spirit and power of Elijah . . . to make ready a people prepared for the Lord'.

Yet when John the Baptist is asked if he is Elijah, his reply is that he is not (John 1:21). How do we make sense of this? It may be that some expected that Elijah would appear in person, and that John is explaining that he is John, not Elijah, even though he has an Elijah-like ministry. Or it may be that John does not yet realize that he has this role. Jesus told his disciples that

'Elijah comes and will restore all things. But I tell you, Elijah has already come, and they did not recognise him, but have done to him everything they wished. In the same way the Son of Man is going to suffer at their hands.' Then the disciples understood that he was talking to them about John the Baptist.
(Matt. 17:11–13)

Elijah has come, in the ministry of John the Baptist, who has indeed prepared the way for the Lord Jesus. But he was rejected and killed, as the Son of Man, Jesus himself, would be rejected and killed. In the words of

Don Carson, 'the Baptist (Elijah) did fulfill his mission, but he was killed doing it. "In the same way the Son of Man is going to suffer . . . at their hands."'[4]

In a different way, we see both Moses and Elijah personally present in the New Testament at the transfiguration of Jesus: 'Just then there appeared before them Moses and Elijah, talking with Jesus.' Moses and Elijah are the representatives of the Old Testament who are present to authenticate Jesus as the Messiah and the Son of God. They witness the words of the Father: 'This is my Son, whom I love; with him I am well pleased. Listen to him!' (Matt. 17:3, 5).

The book of Malachi ends with these words: *or else I will come and strike the land with total destruction* (6). This is such a frightening ending to the book that many Jewish readers would repeat 4:5 after having read 4:6, so as to avoid leaving a nasty sound in the ears of the people. This curse is, as we have seen, the curse of Deuteronomy 28 – 30, and these curses are sent by the Lord to his people when they turn against him, break his covenant, and fail to keep his commands. The distresses of God's people would be manifestations of this curse, if they did not return to God and repent.

As we have already seen from Galatians, Christ bore this curse for his people and for us (Gal. 3:10–14). We see a vivid picture of Christ bearing the curse of God on the cross, as we also see a vivid anticipation of the new life promised in Christ's resurrection, in Matthew's Gospel.

From noon until three in the afternoon darkness came over all the land. About three in the afternoon Jesus cried out in a loud voice, '*Eli, Eli, lema sabachthani?*' (which means 'My God, my God, why have you forsaken me?') . . . And when Jesus had cried out again in a loud voice, he gave up his spirit.

At that moment the curtain of the temple was torn in two from top to bottom. The earth shook, the rocks split and the tombs broke open. The bodies of many holy people who had died were raised to life.
(Matt. 27:45–46, 50–52)

We see here that Jesus bore the curse of God in the darkness that came over the whole land for three hours, and in his cry, 'My God, my God, why

---

4 Carson, 'Matthew', p. 389.

have you forsaken me?' Yet we also see signs of resurrection hope, in the many holy people raised from death, a great sign of the great general resurrection to come, and a great sign of the transformation of the universe at the return of Christ (see Rom. 8:18–25). No wonder some believed: 'When the centurion and those with him who were guarding Jesus saw the earthquake and all that had happened, they were terrified, and exclaimed, "Surely he was the Son of God!"' (Matt. 27:54).

Here is a good warning not to trust in our own righteousness, but in the righteousness of Christ; not in our own service of God, but in the work of Christ, God's servant, on our behalf and in our place (Acts 13:38–39; Rom. 3:21–26; Phil. 3:4–11). Jesus bore the curse of God in our place, and 'God made him who had no sin to be sin for us, so that in him we might become the righteousness of God' (2 Cor. 5:21).

Here too is a good warning to us to die to sin and to live to righteousness (1 Pet. 2:24), to consider ourselves dead to sin but alive to God in Christ, through the power of his death and resurrection (Rom. 6:5–13); to put to death what is earthly, and put on our new life (Col. 3:5–14); and to put off the works of the flesh, and to walk by the Spirit (Gal. 5:16–26). Let us live as those who are free of the curse and judgment of God, and as those who have been set free from the penalty and power of sin by the death and resurrection of Christ, and by the power of the Holy Spirit.

Like the people in Malachi's day, we are called to look back and look forward. We look back to the coming of Christ, and to his incarnation, life, death, resurrection and ascension; and we look forward to the coming of Christ in glory, when he will save his people, judge all people, and restore all things.

And he is the head of the body, the church; he is the beginning and the firstborn from among the dead, so that in everything he might have the supremacy. For God was pleased to have all his fullness dwell in him, and through him to reconcile to himself all things, whether things on earth or things in heaven, by making peace through his blood, shed on the cross.
(Col. 1:18–20)

May we know God's love in the atoning death of Christ: 'But God demonstrates his own love for us in this: while we were still sinners, Christ died for us' (Rom. 5:8);[5] and may we know God's love through the ministry of the Spirit: 'God's love has been poured out into our hearts through the Holy Spirit, who has been given to us' (Rom. 5:5). For, because God is 'for us', nothing 'will be able to separate us from the love of God that is in Christ Jesus our Lord' (Rom. 8:31, 38–39). God says to us: 'I have loved you in the Lord Jesus Christ.' Praise our God and Saviour!

The best remedy against doubting God's love is to continually praise and thank God for his love and mercy to us in the Lord Jesus Christ. Let's join in the great songs of praise in Revelation, the last book of the New Testament:

To him who loves us and has freed us from our sins by his blood, and has made us to be a kingdom and priests to serve his God and Father – to him be glory and power for ever and ever! Amen . . .

Worthy is the Lamb, who was slain,
  to receive power and wealth and wisdom and strength
  and honour and glory and praise! . . .

To him who sits on the throne and to the Lamb
  be praise and honour and glory and power
  for ever and ever!
(Rev. 1:5–6; 5:12–13)

---

[5] See also the close connection between the love of God and the atoning death of Christ in Eph. 1:3–7; 2:4–7; Titus 3:4–7; 1 John 3:16; 4:10, in addition to these references in Romans.

The Bible Speaks Today: Old Testament series

The Bible Speaks Today: New Testament series

The Message of 1 Timothy and Titus
The life of the local church
John Stott

The Message of 2 Timothy
Guard the gospel
John Stott

The Message of Hebrews
Christ above all
Raymond Brown

The Message of James
The tests of faith
Alec Motyer

The Message of 1 Peter
The way of the cross
Edmund Clowney

The Message of 2 Peter and Jude
The promise of his coming
Dick Lucas and Chris Green

The Message of John's Letters
Living in the love of God
David Jackman

The Message of Revelation
I saw heaven opened
Michael Wilcock